Origami Animals

Hector Rojas

Sterling Publishing Co., Inc.   New York

Translated from the German by Elisabeth Reinersmann
Edited by Jeanette Green

Cover photo, photo of materials (pp. 8, 9), and origami photos: all by Michael Zorn, Wiesbaden. Photo layout by Marion Gross, Wiesbaden.

Nature photography:
Dr. Rudolf König, Museum of Zoology of the University of Kiel (p. 129); Ingeborg Polaschek, Linsengericht-Altenhasslau (pp. 20, 24); Reinhard-Tierfoto, Heiligenkreuzsteinach-Eiterbach (pp. 18–19, 26, 31, 36, 40–41, 44, 49, 50–51, 55, 58, 62–63, 67, 72–73, 77, 83, 85, 95, 107, 109, 148–149, 153, 158); Silvestris Fotoservice, Kastl (Pölking: p. 89; Wolfgang Willmer: p. 133); Animal Photo Archive Toni Angermayer, Holskirchen (pp. 84, 100; Hans Pfletschinger: pp. 139, 141; Hans Reinhard: pp. 99, 128; Rudolf Schmidt: p. 94; Zoo Hellbabrun: p. 118; Günther Ziesler: pp. 27, 108, 113, 119, 138).

Drawings by Hector Rojas and Raaf & Gratzfeld Design, Mainz.

Library of Congress Cataloging-in-Publication Data

Rojas, Hector.
    [Faszinierende Origami-Tierwelt. English]
    Origami animals / Hector Rojas.
        p.   cm.
    Includes index.
    ISBN 0-8069-8648-4
    1. Origami.   2. Animals in art.   I. Title.
TT870.R57513   1992
736′.982—dc20   92-18266
                                         CIP

10 9 8 7 6 5 4 3 2

First paperback edition published in 1993 by
Sterling Publishing Company, Inc.
387 Park Avenue South, New York, N.Y. 10016
English translation © 1992 by Sterling Publishing Company, Inc.
Originally published in Germany by Falken-Verlag GmbH
under the title *Faszinierende Origami-Tierwelt*
© 1991 by Falken-Verlag GmbH
Distributed in Canada by Sterling Publishing
% Canadian Manda Group, P.O. Box 920, Station U
Toronto, Ontario, Canada M8Z 5P9
Distributed in Great Britain and Europe by Cassell PLC
Villiers House, 41/47 Strand, London WC2N 5JE, England
Distributed in Australia by Capricorn Link Ltd.
P.O. Box 665, Lane Cove, NSW 2066
Printed and bound in Hong Kong
All rights reserved

Sterling ISBN 0-8069-8648-4 Trade
            0-8069-8649-2 Paper

Contents

Introduction

I spent my childhood in La Paz, the capital of Bolivia. As children, we learned early how to use our imagination to create our own playthings, since our parents could not afford ready-made toys. We made do with the few things we had—paper, cardboard, boxes, and empty cans. Inspiration came not just from looking into store display windows, but also from observing the natural environment we loved, respected, and lived in. During those early years I created my first animals by folding paper forms.

Origami

Only much later, when I arrived in Europe, did I learn about *origami*, the ancient Japanese art of paper-folding that dates back to the 9th century. Origami probably originated in the traditional good-luck charms that were folded and attached to wrapped presents. Over the centuries, paper-folding became a distinct art form that found many different expressions and uses, and it eventually found its way into other cultures. Most origami shapes and figures have been inspired by the plant and animal worlds.

Re-creating Nature

The book provides detailed drawings for the process of paper-folding, and colored photos of live animals remain close by for inspiration when re-creating the animal in paper. Using nature as the model for creating origami forms makes this creative hobby into a wonderful way to learn about animals, plants, and the environment we live in. For me, origami is a way of dedicating myself to nature—almost a way of preserving natural forms—and capturing the images of life.

I hope that this book will not simply provide models for creating origami shapes and forms, but that it will also help stimulate appreciation of the beauty of nature. Since nature has been so seriously threatened by environmental hazards, I hope these pages will not just stir your imagination, but encourage you to actively protect our environment and all the living creatures in it.

Folding Tips

- When folding paper, it is essential to work with great care, making sure that edges and corners are exactly on top of each other.
- The more precise your folds, the better your finished animal will look.
- Go over a crease with a fingernail to reinforce your fold.
- Before beginning to fold, study drawings carefully, and read the instructions as you would any book text.
- Each drawing shows the result of the previous fold and gives directions for the next fold.
- After completing a folding sequence, return the figure to the correct starting position.

- If you encounter difficulties, retrace the previous two steps, and compare your work with the drawing and instructions. Reread them until you solve the problem.
- Origami consists of so-called basic forms from which several different animals can be created. See the dragon (drawing 20, page 10).
- Many forms can take on different shapes by simply making small changes in the position of an animal's body. See, for instance, the giraffe and flamingo sections.

Material, Colors, and Decoration

Many different kinds of paper, like typewriter or gift wrap paper, are suitable for folding. However, in the beginning many people recommend using proper origami paper. Origami paper is sold already cut into true squares, and since each side has a different color, it would be easier to keep track of the folding sequences described in this book.

Other accessories include scissors; an X-acto knife, if possible; a ruler that becomes a paper cutting guide when used with an X-acto knife; tweezers; paper glue for complicated animal forms; and pointed pliers to aid folding several layers of paper.

Animals folded from plain paper can be painted with watercolors or wallpaper paint. Use brushes of several different sizes; also try crayons and felt-tip pens for coloring animals. The original photos of live animals in this book are a good guide for selecting colors. It is also helpful to ob-

serve animals when you visit the zoo or when you see them in their natural environment.

Things to be used for decoration can be found almost everywhere—in the woods, park, or yard. For instance, leaves, small twigs, bark, and parts from very young trees, acorns, chestnuts, bird feathers, small stones, moss, straw, grasses, dried mushrooms, and wheat grass are useful. When you're on vacation at the beach, look for shells, corals, and particularly beautiful stones. In hobby stores, find model trains, blue foil to create a waterfall, green foil for artificial turf, and coarse powder to cover edges. In pet stores, you'll see artificial algae, gravel, stones, and slate. In flower shops or nurseries, you can find dried flowers, grasses, and moss.

In addition, handcrafted items made from paper, cartons, wire, and crêpe paper may come in handy.

Basic Forms

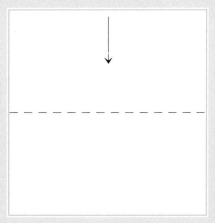

1. Fold a square of paper horizontally on the dashed line.

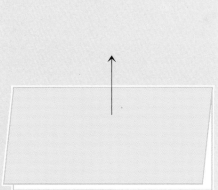

2. Unfold the paper.

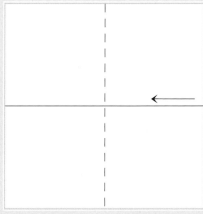

3. Fold the paper vertically from right to left, as shown.

Pocket Crab

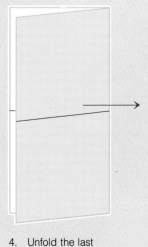

4. Unfold the last fold.

5. Turn the paper over.

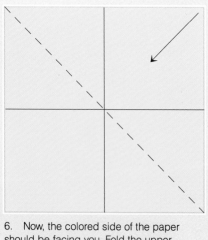

6.   Now, the colored side of the paper should be facing you. Fold the upper right corner down to the lower left corner on the dashed line.

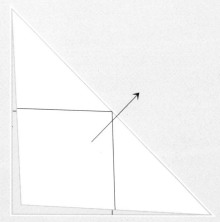

7.   Unfold the last fold.

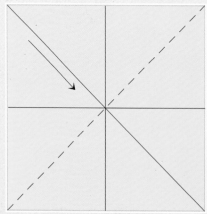

8.   Fold the opposite diagonal on the dashed line.

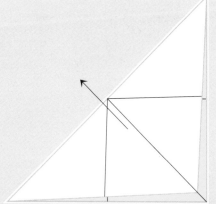

9.   Unfold the last fold.

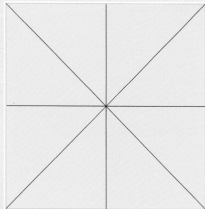

10.   Turn the paper over.

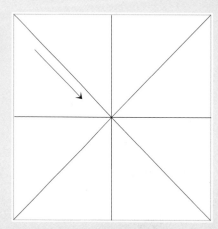

11.   Now the white side of the paper should be facing you. Fold the upper left corner diagonally to the lower right corner.

Symbols

– – – – A dashed line indicates where to fold the paper.	✂ Scissors indicate that you need to make a cut or to cut off part of the paper.
——— A solid line indicates a crease already present and used for the next fold.	→ ← Arrows indicate the direction of the next fold.
○→ Turn over the paper or figure before making the next fold.	↖ ↗ Diverging arrows indicate that you fold a corner of the figure toward the outside.

Two curved arrows indicate that you fold a corner of the figure to the inside.

A single curved arrow indicates that you rotate the figure on your work surface 180 degrees.

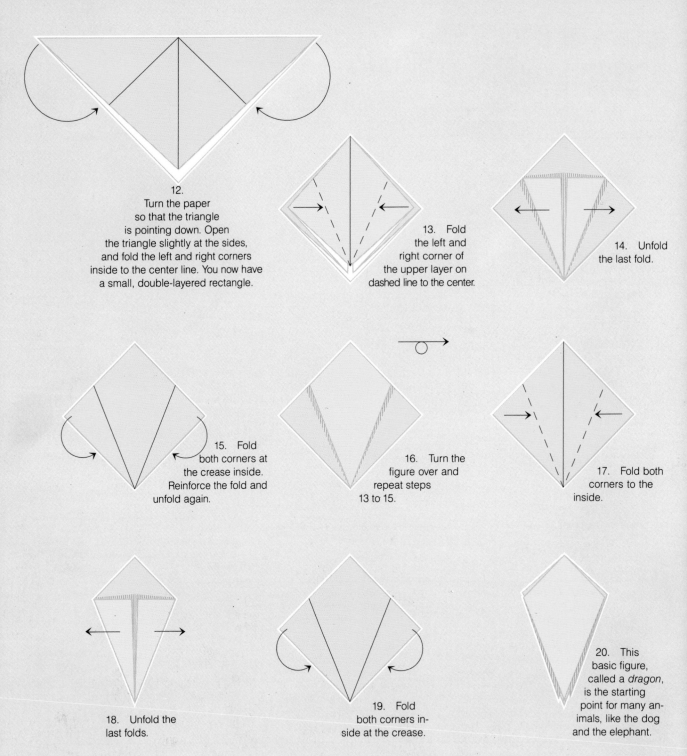

12.
Turn the paper
so that the triangle
is pointing down. Open
the triangle slightly at the sides,
and fold the left and right corners
inside to the center line. You now have
a small, double-layered rectangle.

13.   Fold
the left and
right corner of
the upper layer on
dashed line to the center.

14.   Unfold
the last fold.

15.   Fold
both corners at
the crease inside.
Reinforce the fold and
unfold again.

16.   Turn the
figure over and
repeat steps
13 to 15.

17.   Fold both
corners to the
inside.

18.   Unfold the
last folds.

19.   Fold
both corners in-
side at the crease.

20.   This
basic figure,
called a *dragon*,
is the starting
point for many an-
imals, like the dog
and the elephant.

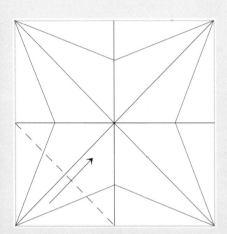

21. Completely unfold the whole dragon figure, with the white side facing you. Fold the lower left and right corners to the center.

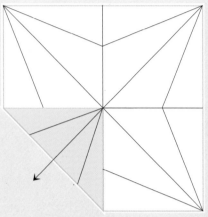

22. Unfold the last fold.

Tarantula

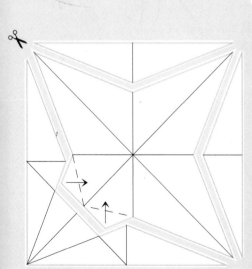

23. Cut the shape according to sketch as shown. Fold both corners at the cut-off corner, inside along dashed line.

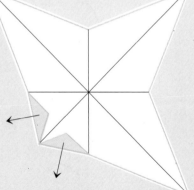

24. Unfold the last fold.

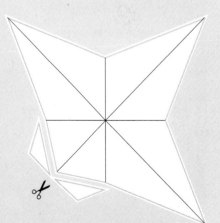

25. Cut off those two corners at the crease. This is also the starting point, or basic form, for many other animals, like the flamingo.

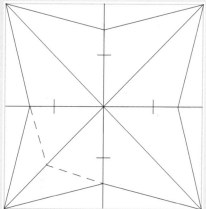

26. To make this figure, follow directions for the basic form—steps 1 to 21. However, at step 13, both corners should be only folded halfway, *not* all the way, to the center line. This will create a star with a wider point.

27. Cut the figure according to the sketch, snipping off the lower left corner.

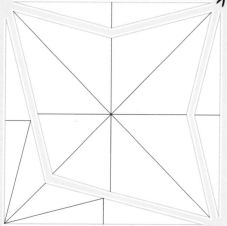

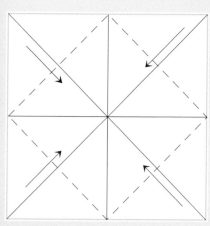

28. This figure is the starting point for the toucan.

Toucans in a Paper Wood Jungle

29. Fold and crease all four corners to the center.

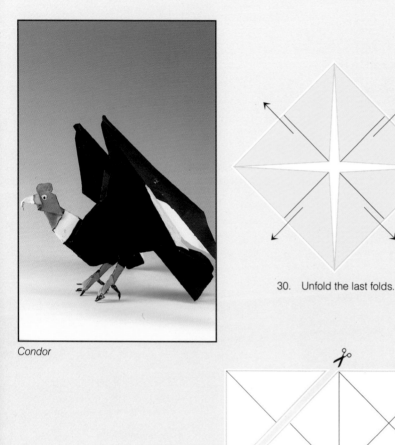

Condor

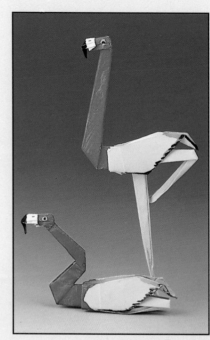

30.   Unfold the last folds.

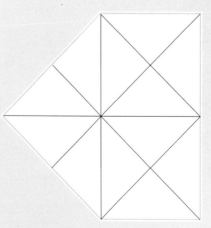

Flamingos

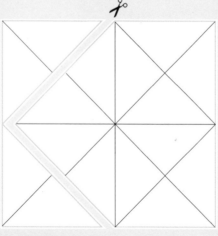

32.   Cut off the upper and lower left corners as shown.

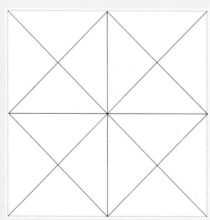

31.   This is what your figure should look like.

33.   This basic form is the figure you begin with when making many different birds, like the condor.

Turtle

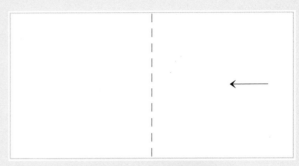

34.   Fold a rectangular piece of paper (that's twice as long as it is wide) vertically at the dashed line.

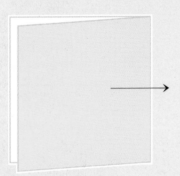

35.   Unfold the last fold.

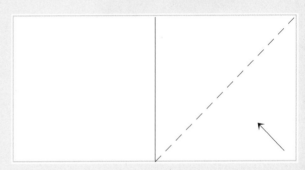

36.   Fold the lower right corner diagonally to the middle.

37.   Unfold the last fold.

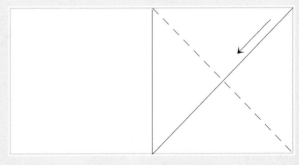

38.   Fold the upper right corner diagonally to the middle.

39. Unfold the last fold.

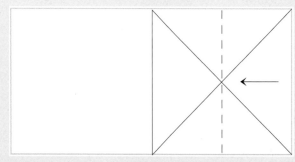

40. Fold the right half of the rectangle at the dashed line to the middle.

41. Unfold the last fold.

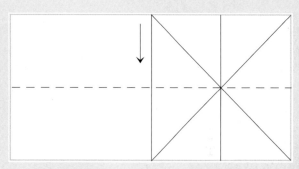

42. Fold the rectangle horizontally in half at the dashed line.

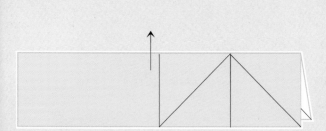

43. Unfold the last fold.

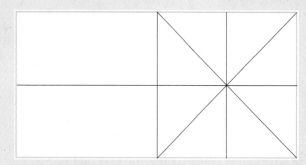

44. This is the basic form for the turtle.

For over 10,000 years, dogs have served as protectors and hunting companions for people, aiding in their struggle to survive. Dogs have in common with intelligent, and often dangerous, wolves highly developed senses of hearing and smell. Many domestic species developed over the centuries have contributed to more than 400 different breeds we know today. They are divided, according to their special skills, into four basic categories—shepherd and watch dogs, hunting dogs, guide dogs, and greyhounds. Today, dogs are one of the most loved house pets. Some people insist that a master and his or her dog seem to develop similar personality traits over time. One reason for the closeness between humans and dogs is that their emotions seem much alike; only in the intensity of emotions do dogs remain a world ahead of us. That holds true for dogs' sadness and joy, as well as their fear, hope, and desire. But humans love canine companions most for their loyalty, devotion, alertness, and protective instinct.

Basset Hound

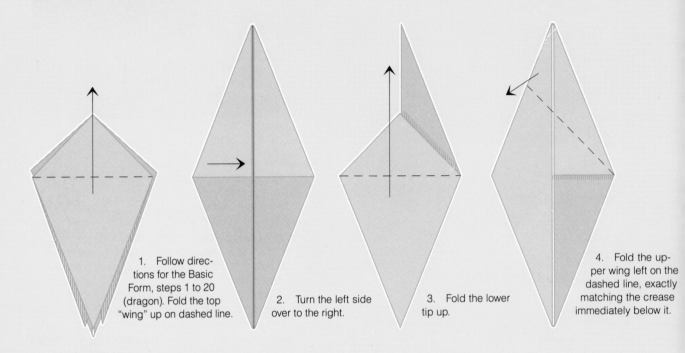

1. Follow directions for the Basic Form, steps 1 to 20 (dragon). Fold the top "wing" up on dashed line.

2. Turn the left side over to the right.

3. Fold the lower tip up.

4. Fold the upper wing left on the dashed line, exactly matching the crease immediately below it.

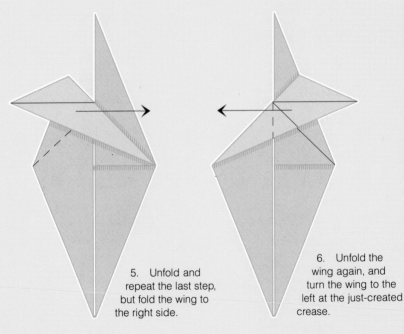

5. Unfold and repeat the last step, but fold the wing to the right side.

6. Unfold the wing again, and turn the wing to the left at the just-created crease.

Characteristic of a basset hound are his "melancholy face"; a long, straight back; and a pronounced nose.

A basset hound is not suitable for hunting, but he loves daily walks as long as they don't turn into extended hikes.

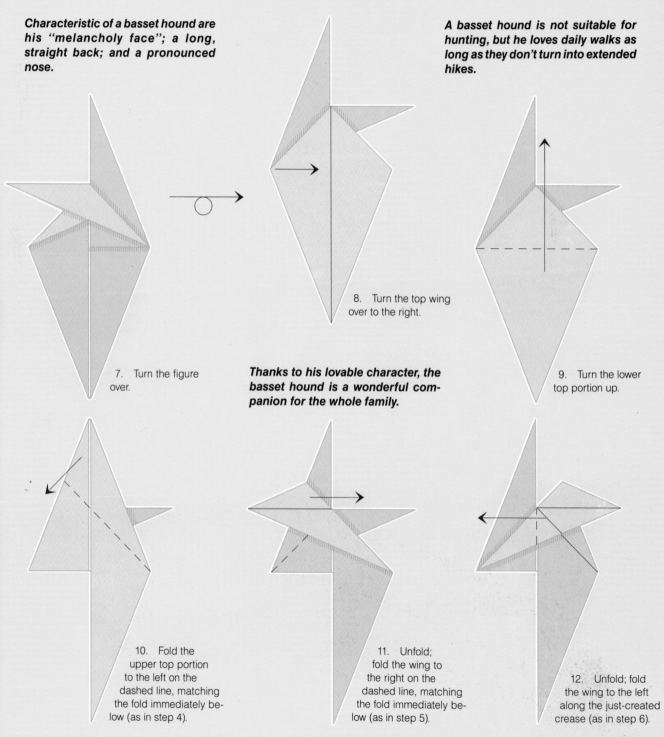

7.   Turn the figure over.

8.   Turn the top wing over to the right.

9.   Turn the lower top portion up.

Thanks to his lovable character, the basset hound is a wonderful companion for the whole family.

10.   Fold the upper top portion to the left on the dashed line, matching the fold immediately below (as in step 4).

11.   Unfold; fold the wing to the right on the dashed line, matching the fold immediately below (as in step 5).

12.   Unfold; fold the wing to the left along the just-created crease (as in step 6).

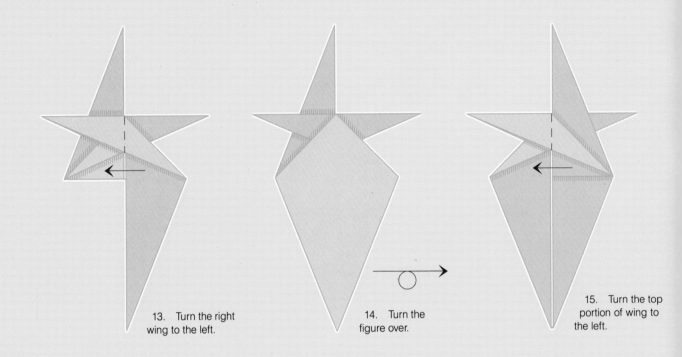

13. Turn the right wing to the left.

14. Turn the figure over.

15. Turn the top portion of wing to the left.

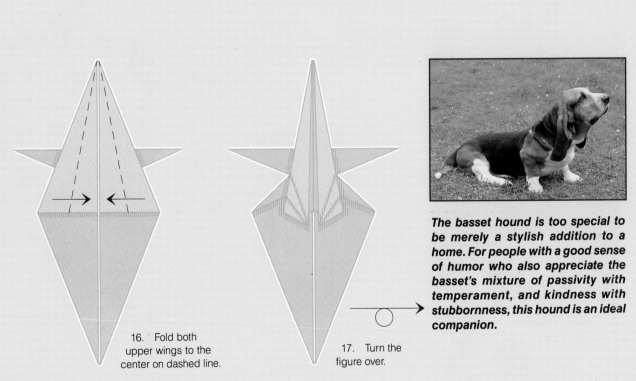

16. Fold both upper wings to the center on dashed line.

17. Turn the figure over.

The basset hound is too special to be merely a stylish addition to a home. For people with a good sense of humor who also appreciate the basset's mixture of passivity with temperament, and kindness with stubbornness, this hound is an ideal companion.

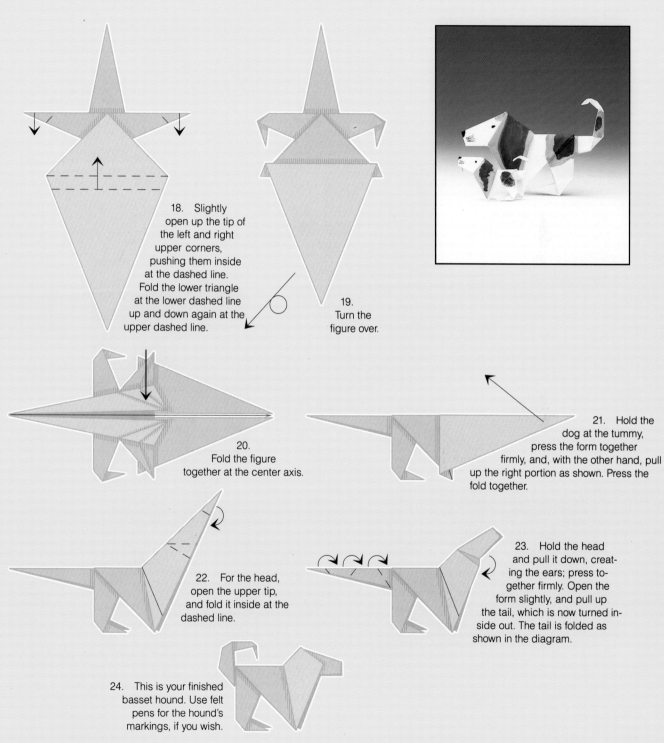

18. Slightly open up the tip of the left and right upper corners, pushing them inside at the dashed line. Fold the lower triangle at the lower dashed line up and down again at the upper dashed line.

19. Turn the figure over.

20. Fold the figure together at the center axis.

21. Hold the dog at the tummy, press the form together firmly, and, with the other hand, pull up the right portion as shown. Press the fold together.

22. For the head, open the upper tip, and fold it inside at the dashed line.

23. Hold the head and pull it down, creating the ears; press together firmly. Open the form slightly, and pull up the tail, which is now turned inside out. The tail is folded as shown in the diagram.

24. This is your finished basset hound. Use felt pens for the hound's markings, if you wish.

An elephant's large ears protect him against the sun and are used like a fan. With his trunk, an extension of his nose, an elephant can smell and feel, as well as grab and carry food to his mouth and make trumpet-like sounds. He also uses it to give himself a refreshing shower or to chase away people who annoy him. His tusks, which furnish precious ivory, grow continuously throughout his life and become a handy tool. He often uses them as a crowbar, and, if necessary, they can also become a weapon. The body of this usually peaceful, immense pachyderm is supported by column-like legs with short, wide feet. He moves with spring-like steps in spite of his enormous weight and size, due to the elastic pads on the soles of his feet. The elephant is the largest land animal. Two kinds of elephants inhabit the earth—the African and the Indian, or Asian, elephant. The African elephant, the larger of the two, grows up to 11 feet (4 meters) tall, and can weigh over 8 tons. He lives in the steppes, savannas, and woodlands in the African continent south of the Sahara. The Indian elephant lives in India and the remains of rain forests in Southeast Asia and Indonesia. He is in great danger of extinction—much more so than his African counterpart.

Baby Elephant

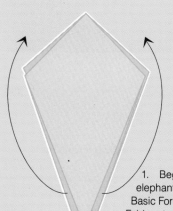

1. Begin the baby elephant by using the Basic Form, steps 1 to 20. Fold up two "wings" as shown.

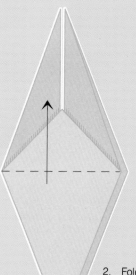

2. Fold the bottom wing up to the upper corner.

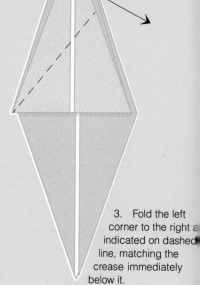

3. Fold the left corner to the right as indicated on dashed line, matching the crease immediately below it.

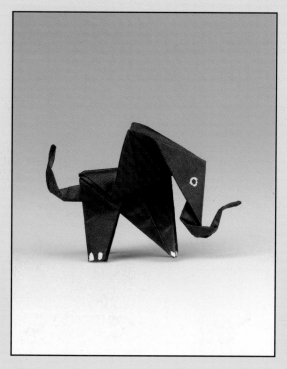

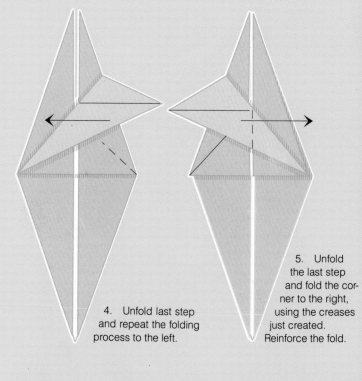

4. Unfold last step and repeat the folding process to the left.

5. Unfold the last step and fold the corner to the right, using the creases just created. Reinforce the fold.

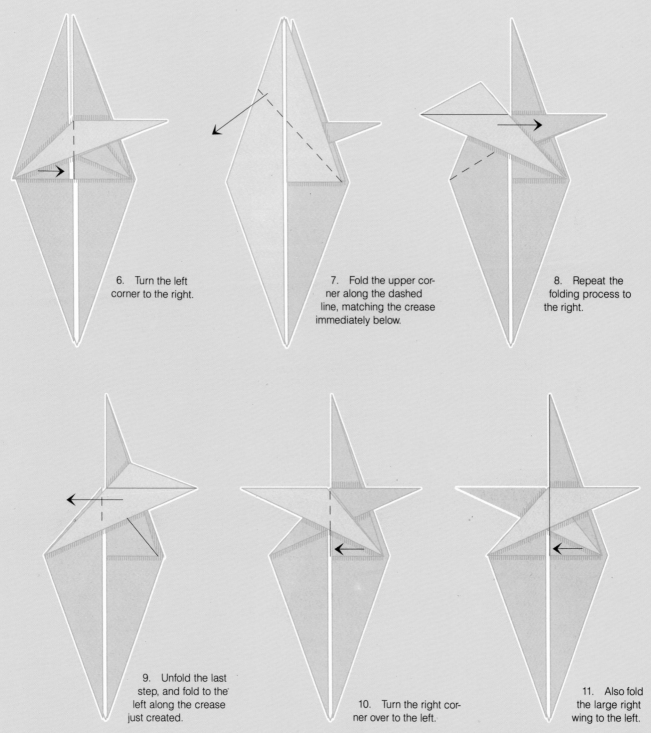

6. Turn the left corner to the right.

7. Fold the upper corner along the dashed line, matching the crease immediately below.

8. Repeat the folding process to the right.

9. Unfold the last step, and fold to the left along the crease just created.

10. Turn the right corner over to the left.

11. Also fold the large right wing to the left.

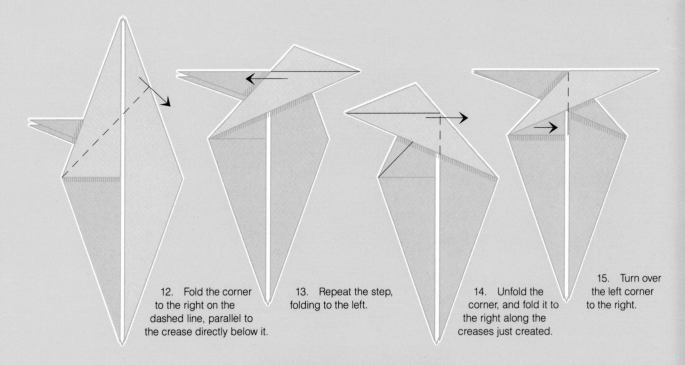

12. Fold the corner to the right on the dashed line, parallel to the crease directly below it.

13. Repeat the step, folding to the left.

14. Unfold the corner, and fold it to the right along the creases just created.

15. Turn over the left corner to the right.

In the past, more than one hundred elephants made up a herd, but to-day's herds have, at best, one-third that number.

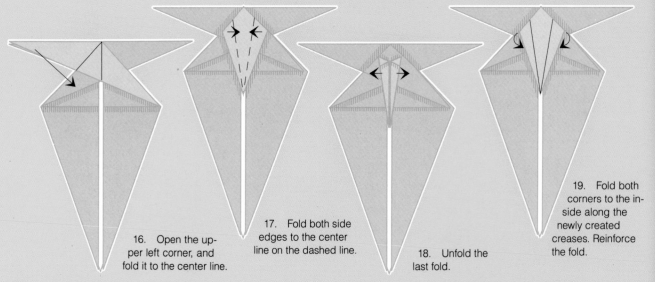

16. Open the up-per left corner, and fold it to the center line.

17. Fold both side edges to the center line on the dashed line.

18. Unfold the last fold.

19. Fold both corners to the in-side along the newly created creases. Reinforce the fold.

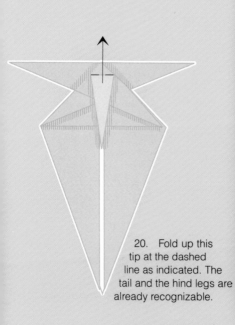

20. Fold up this tip at the dashed line as indicated. The tail and the hind legs are already recognizable.

Baby African elephant taking a bath

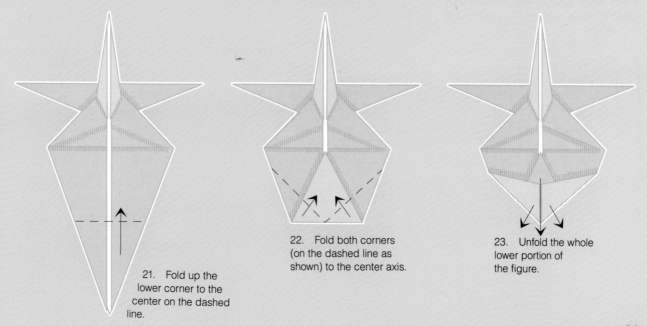

21. Fold up the lower corner to the center on the dashed line.

22. Fold both corners (on the dashed line as shown) to the center axis.

23. Unfold the whole lower portion of the figure.

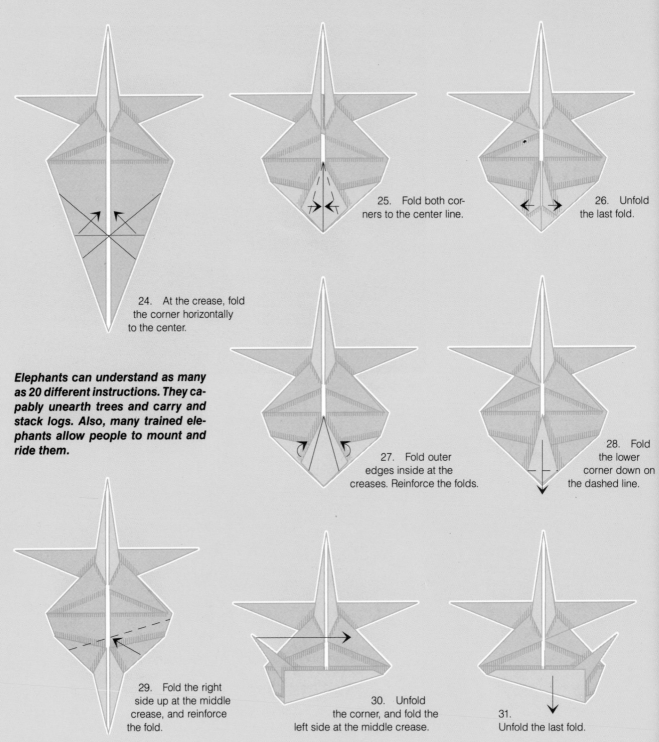

24.   At the crease, fold the corner horizontally to the center.

Elephants can understand as many as 20 different instructions. They capably unearth trees and carry and stack logs. Also, many trained elephants allow people to mount and ride them.

25.   Fold both corners to the center line.

26.   Unfold the last fold.

27.   Fold outer edges inside at the creases. Reinforce the folds.

28.   Fold the lower corner down on the dashed line.

29.   Fold the right side up at the middle crease, and reinforce the fold.

30.   Unfold the corner, and fold the left side at the middle crease.

31. Unfold the last fold.

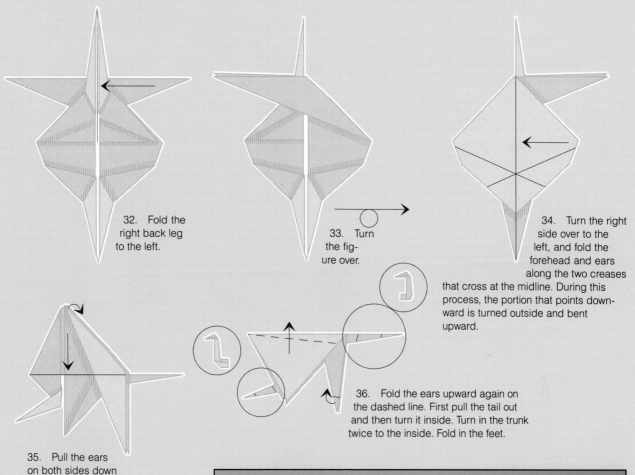

32. Fold the right back leg to the left.

33. Turn the figure over.

34. Turn the right side over to the left, and fold the forehead and ears along the two creases that cross at the midline. During this process, the portion that points downward is turned outside and bent upward.

35. Pull the ears on both sides down over the middle axis.

36. Fold the ears upward again on the dashed line. First pull the tail out and then turn it inside. Turn in the trunk twice to the inside. Fold in the feet.

37. This is the finished baby elephant.

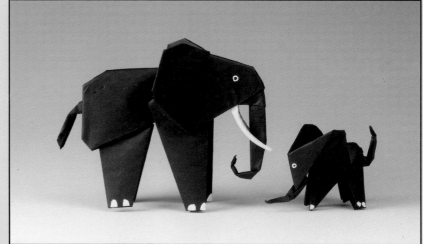

Adult Elephant

Hindquarters

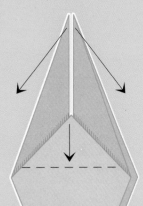

Elephants live as long as 60 or 70 years. In their search for food they travel great distances nightly. An elephant needs from 600 to 1,000 pounds (270 to 454 kilograms) of vegetation each day.

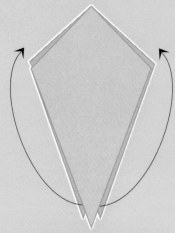

1. For the elephant's hindquarters, fold Basic Form, steps 1 to 20. Fold up and crease both side "wings" of the dragon figure.

2. Pull down both upper wings into a horizontal position and press them together. Fold down the top corner on the dashed line.

3. Fold the lower corner up on dashed line to match the left wing.

4. Unfold the last step, and repeat step 3 to the right.

5. Unfold the last step, and press it into place so that it becomes an extension of the center axis. This will later become the tail.

34

For centuries, elephants in India have been trained to perform important work. African elephants, which are just as intelligent, have rarely been trained.

6. Fold both parts of the tail to the middle.

7. Fold the figure together at the middle, and turn it 90 degrees.

8. Pull the tail slightly down, and press it into place.

9. This is how your figure should look.

10. Turn the upper right corner inside on the dashed line. Turn the tail down, and turn the tips of the feet inside.

Although the ivory trade has been banned in most countries, the killing of elephants for ivory has increased at an alarming rate.

11. The hindquarters are finished.

Front Portion

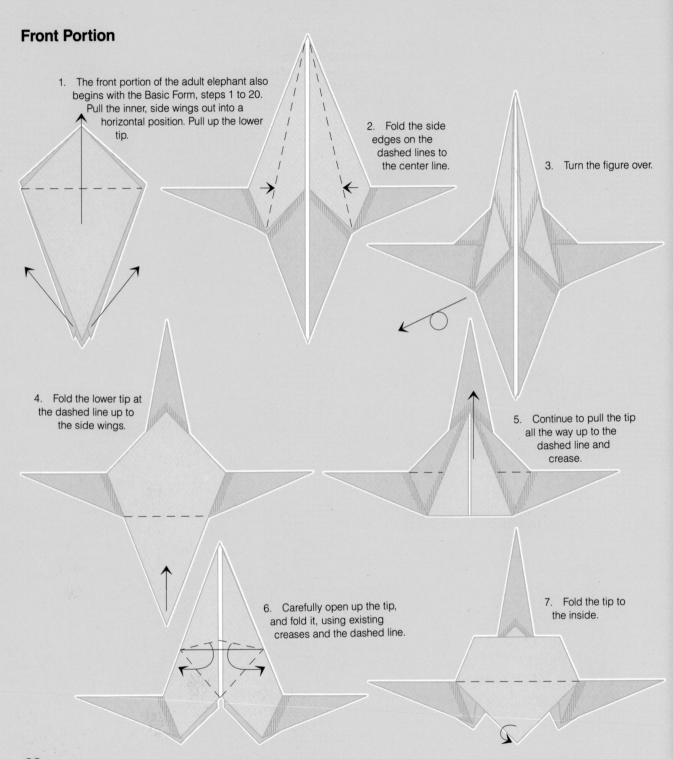

1. The front portion of the adult elephant also begins with the Basic Form, steps 1 to 20. Pull the inner, side wings out into a horizontal position. Pull up the lower tip.

2. Fold the side edges on the dashed lines to the center line.

3. Turn the figure over.

4. Fold the lower tip at the dashed line up to the side wings.

5. Continue to pull the tip all the way up to the dashed line and crease.

6. Carefully open up the tip, and fold it, using existing creases and the dashed line.

7. Fold the tip to the inside.

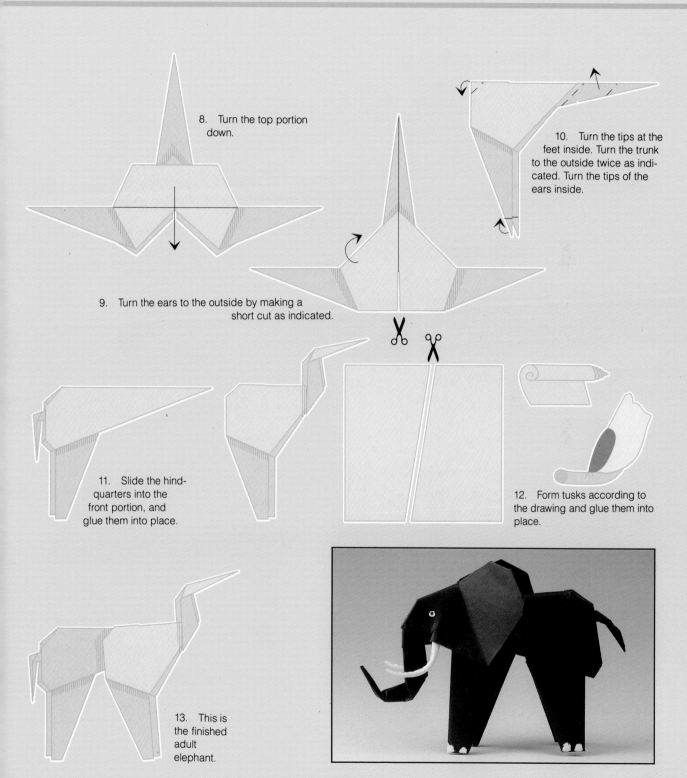

8.   Turn the top portion down.

9.   Turn the ears to the outside by making a short cut as indicated.

10.   Turn the tips at the feet inside. Turn the trunk to the outside twice as indicated. Turn the tips of the ears inside.

11.   Slide the hindquarters into the front portion, and glue them into place.

12.   Form tusks according to the drawing and glue them into place.

13.   This is the finished adult elephant.

The most striking feature of the male lion is his immense mane, something that is missing in the female. This most congenial of all big cats originally lived throughout Africa, in southern Europe, and in Asia as far west as northern and central India. Today they are only found in the semi-deserts, savannas, and steppes of Africa. Their diminished numbers inhabit protected regions of northern and western India. In ancient times, the lion, "king of the beasts," was a symbol of nobility and god-like power, as depicted in the Egyptian sphinx. But the lion has also been widely used in the West as a heraldic animal, symbolizing power and might. The male lion seems to be the embodiment of strength, but he lives a rather quiet and sedentary life. As the leader of the pack, the male does not need to exert much effort. Almost without fail, females provide the food and give him first choice—the "lion's share," as it were. Only after the male lion has satisfied his appetite will the female lions begin to eat, followed by the younger members of the pack. Generally, lions are strictly carnivorous. Their prey includes mostly antelopes and zebras. During a hunt, the members of a pack—who are usually related to each other—band together when stalking their prey. They are fast sprinters, reaching up to 60 miles per hour, but not long-distance runners. However, prey that a lion has not caught within 165 to 330 feet (50 to 100 metres) has a good chance of escaping. After that, a lioness will run out of air, due to her weight and size.

Lion

Hindquarters

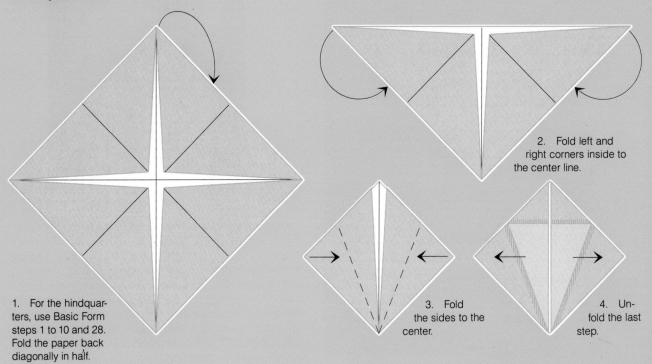

1. For the hindquarters, use Basic Form steps 1 to 10 and 28. Fold the paper back diagonally in half.

2. Fold left and right corners inside to the center line.

3. Fold the sides to the center.

4. Unfold the last step.

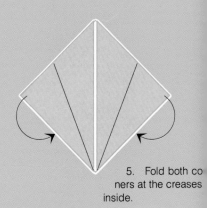

5. Fold both corners at the creases inside.

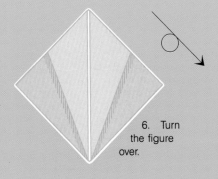

6. Turn the figure over.

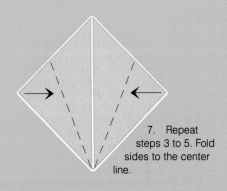

7. Repeat steps 3 to 5. Fold sides to the center line.

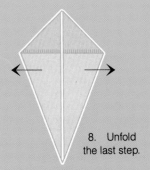

8. Unfold the last step.

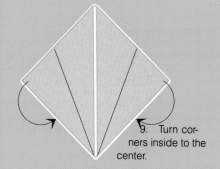

9. Turn corners inside to the center.

Most male lions dominate a pride for only about two or three years. After that, the ruling lion is usually driven away by rivals.

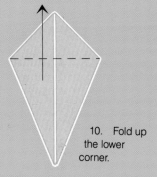

10. Fold up the lower corner.

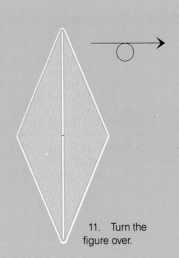

11. Turn the figure over.

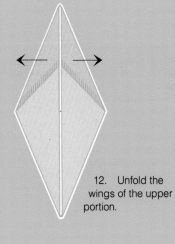

12. Unfold the wings of the upper portion.

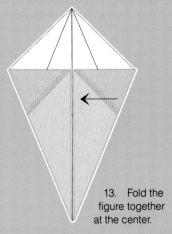

13. Fold the figure together at the center.

Lions do not roar during the hunt. Lions roar, instead, to mark the pride's territorial boundaries.

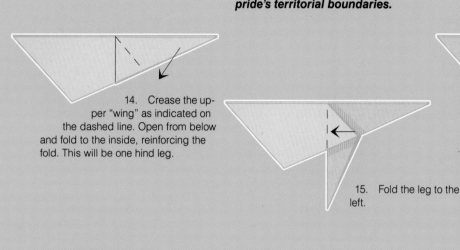

14. Crease the upper "wing" as indicated on the dashed line. Open from below and fold to the inside, reinforcing the fold. This will be one hind leg.

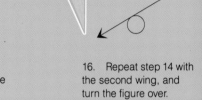

15. Fold the leg to the left.

16. Repeat step 14 with the second wing, and turn the figure over.

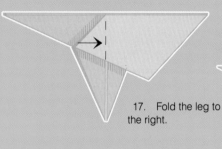

17. Fold the leg to the right.

18. Fold the left corner down on dashed line and turn it inside. Turn the lower tip inside to form the foot.

19. Crease the second hind leg. Turn the hind portion at the crease inside.

A lion with a full stomach becomes lazy, and an animal that would usually become his prey can graze peacefully in his presence.

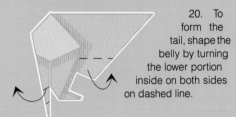

20. To form the tail, shape the belly by turning the lower portion inside on both sides on dashed line.

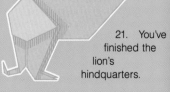

21. You've finished the lion's hindquarters.

Front Portion

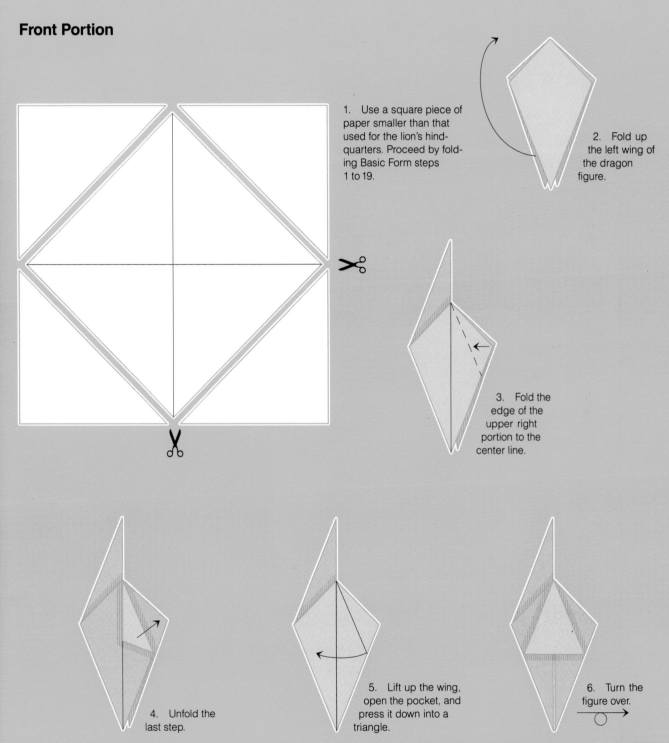

1. Use a square piece of paper smaller than that used for the lion's hind-quarters. Proceed by folding Basic Form steps 1 to 19.

2. Fold up the left wing of the dragon figure.

3. Fold the edge of the upper right portion to the center line.

4. Unfold the last step.

5. Lift up the wing, open the pocket, and press it down into a triangle.

6. Turn the figure over.

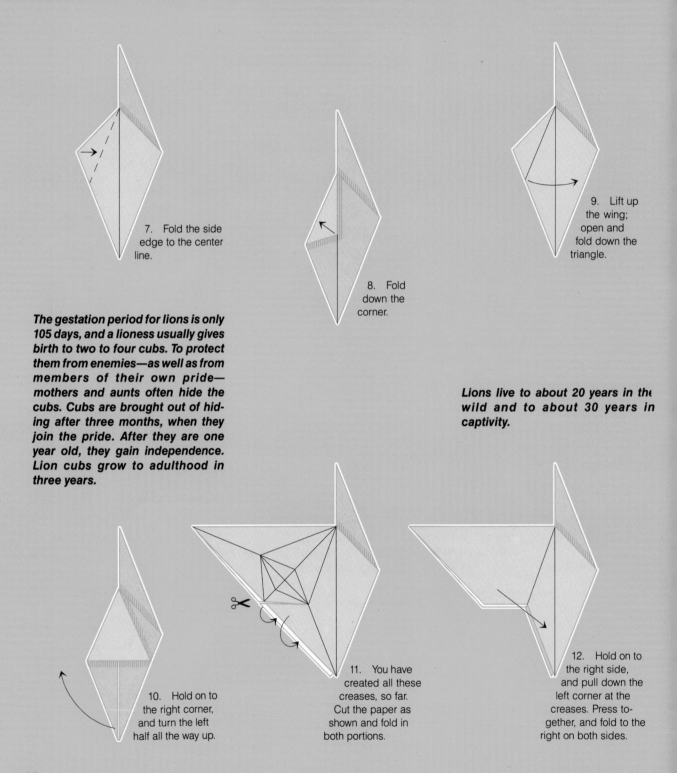

7. Fold the side edge to the center line.

8. Fold down the corner.

9. Lift up the wing; open and fold down the triangle.

The gestation period for lions is only 105 days, and a lioness usually gives birth to two to four cubs. To protect them from enemies—as well as from members of their own pride—mothers and aunts often hide the cubs. Cubs are brought out of hiding after three months, when they join the pride. After they are one year old, they gain independence. Lion cubs grow to adulthood in three years.

Lions live to about 20 years in the wild and to about 30 years in captivity.

10. Hold on to the right corner, and turn the left half all the way up.

11. You have created all these creases, so far. Cut the paper as shown and fold in both portions.

12. Hold on to the right side, and pull down the left corner at the creases. Press together, and fold to the right on both sides.

13. Hold on to the upper tip, pull it down, and push it into the slightly opened lower portion. Press together where marked. Turn the lower tip inside to form the first front leg.

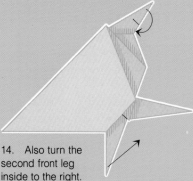

14. Also turn the second front leg inside to the right. Turn the upper tip inside as marked; it becomes the lion's mouth.

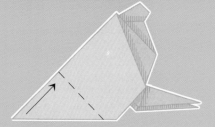

15. Fold up the left wing.

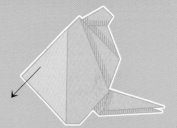

16. Unfold the last step.

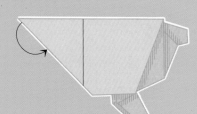

17. Turn the left corner inside as indicated. Fold the right front paw.

18. To form the mane, turn the left corner to the inside. A triangle cut will create the ears.

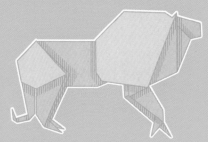

19. Push front and hindquarters together, and glue them in place for your finished lion.

47

Adult giraffes, with a height ranging from 13 to nearly 19 feet (4 to 6 meters), can easily observe wide areas of their terrain. They detect enemies early, and warn friends in time for them to escape potential danger. That's why only very young giraffes may be threatened by a lion attack. However, baby giraffes are fiercely defended by their mothers. Long giraffe legs and hooves can be deadly. Only in the dark are giraffes nearly helpless against a predator, which is why they hardly sleep at all during the night and are often found dozing for hours during the day. Giraffes live in the dry steppes and bushes of Africa, south of the Sahara Desert. In years past, giraffes were widely dispersed over the whole African continent, but since they have been hunted for their fur, whole populations have been totally eradicated in many regions. Giraffe fur is strikingly marked with large spots on a leather-like background. The many different giraffe types can be distinguished by their coloring and the number of bone formations on the head.

Giraffe

Body

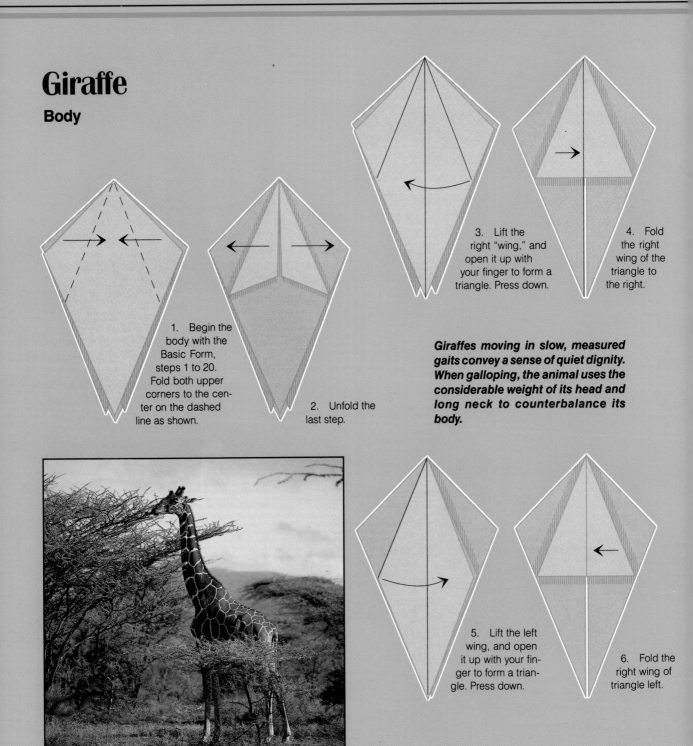

1. Begin the body with the Basic Form, steps 1 to 20. Fold both upper corners to the center on the dashed line as shown.

2. Unfold the last step.

3. Lift the right "wing," and open it up with your finger to form a triangle. Press down.

4. Fold the right wing of the triangle to the right.

Giraffes moving in slow, measured gaits convey a sense of quiet dignity. When galloping, the animal uses the considerable weight of its head and long neck to counterbalance its body.

5. Lift the left wing, and open it up with your finger to form a triangle. Press down.

6. Fold the right wing of triangle left.

50

Since they can see predators from a great distance, giraffes can warn other animals. Some zoologists speculate that giraffes produce infrasonic warning signals.

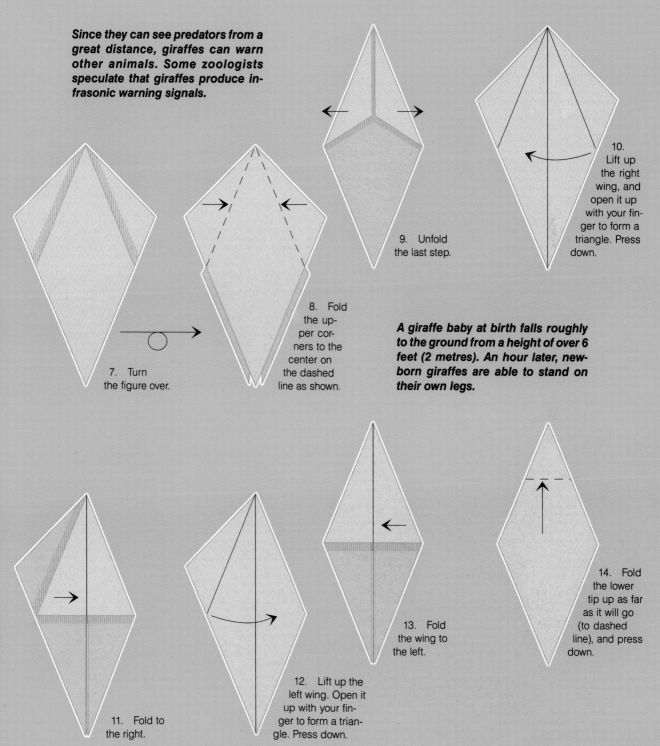

7. Turn the figure over.

8. Fold the upper corners to the center on the dashed line as shown.

9. Unfold the last step.

10. Lift up the right wing, and open it up with your finger to form a triangle. Press down.

A giraffe baby at birth falls roughly to the ground from a height of over 6 feet (2 metres). An hour later, newborn giraffes are able to stand on their own legs.

11. Fold to the right.

12. Lift up the left wing. Open it up with your finger to form a triangle. Press down.

13. Fold the wing to the left.

14. Fold the lower tip up as far as it will go (to dashed line), and press down.

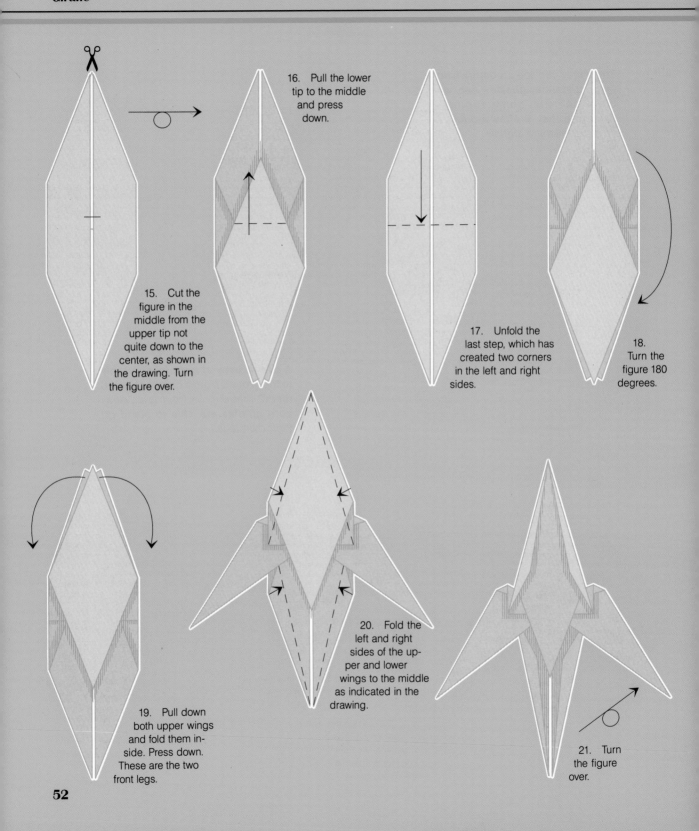

15. Cut the figure in the middle from the upper tip not quite down to the center, as shown in the drawing. Turn the figure over.

16. Pull the lower tip to the middle and press down.

17. Unfold the last step, which has created two corners in the left and right sides.

18. Turn the figure 180 degrees.

19. Pull down both upper wings and fold them inside. Press down. These are the two front legs.

20. Fold the left and right sides of the upper and lower wings to the middle as indicated in the drawing.

21. Turn the figure over.

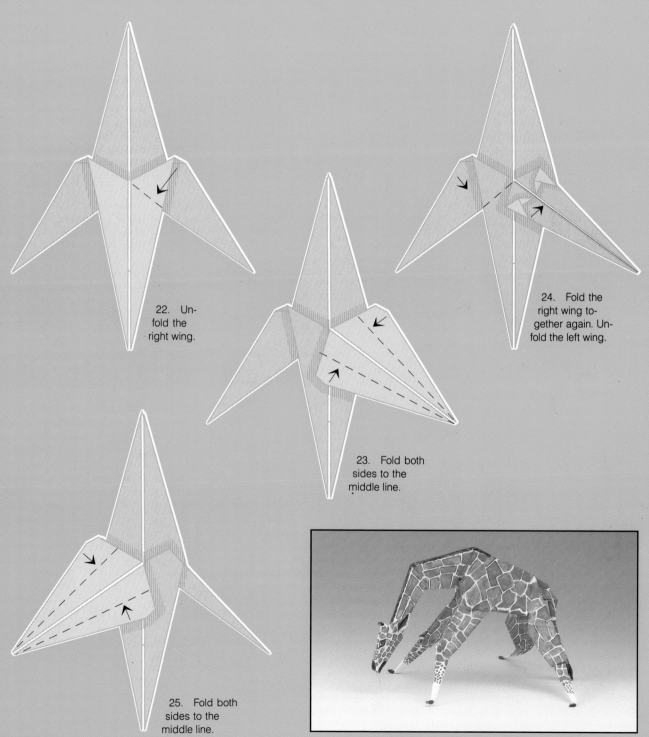

22. Un-fold the right wing.

23. Fold both sides to the middle line.

24. Fold the right wing to-gether again. Un-fold the left wing.

25. Fold both sides to the middle line.

26. Fold the left lower wing flap up, along the middle.

27. Crease the tips of the lower wing, and turn them to the outside on dashed line.

28. Fold the figure together at the center axis.

29. Make a few harmonica folds at the hind legs so that they match the height of the front legs.

Head

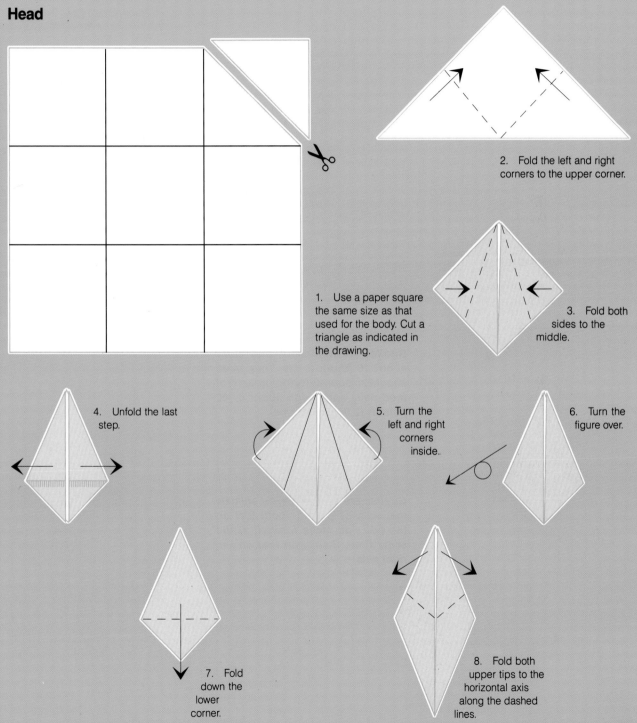

2. Fold the left and right corners to the upper corner.

1. Use a paper square the same size as that used for the body. Cut a triangle as indicated in the drawing.

3. Fold both sides to the middle.

4. Unfold the last step.

5. Turn the left and right corners inside.

6. Turn the figure over.

7. Fold down the lower corner.

8. Fold both upper tips to the horizontal axis along the dashed lines.

57

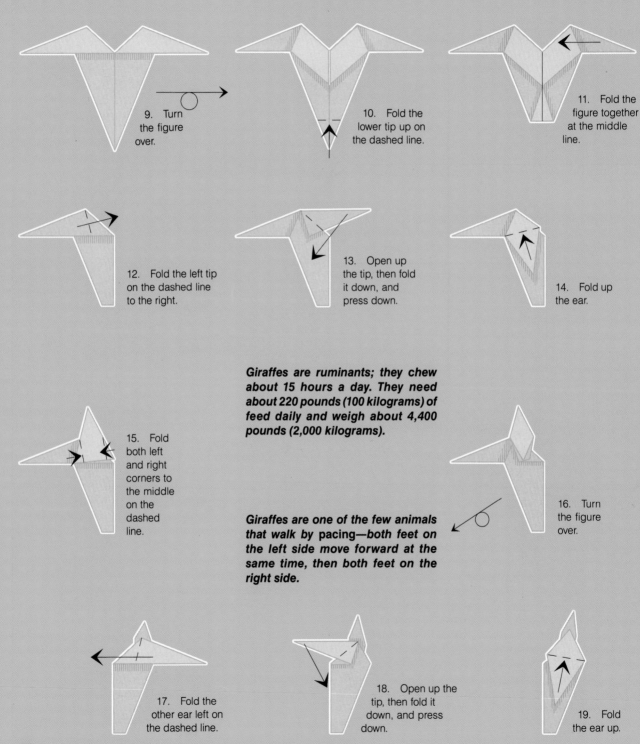

9. Turn the figure over.

10. Fold the lower tip up on the dashed line.

11. Fold the figure together at the middle line.

12. Fold the left tip on the dashed line to the right.

13. Open up the tip, then fold it down, and press down.

14. Fold up the ear.

15. Fold both left and right corners to the middle on the dashed line.

Giraffes are ruminants; they chew about 15 hours a day. They need about 220 pounds (100 kilograms) of feed daily and weigh about 4,400 pounds (2,000 kilograms).

Giraffes are one of the few animals that walk by pacing—both feet on the left side move forward at the same time, then both feet on the right side.

16. Turn the figure over.

17. Fold the other ear left on the dashed line.

18. Open up the tip, then fold it down, and press down.

19. Fold the ear up.

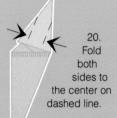

20. Fold both sides to the center on dashed line.

21. Attach the head with glue to the body. Note that the end of the neck protrudes slightly above the head.

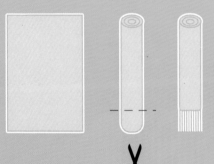

22. For the tail, roll up tightly a small, rectangular piece of paper. At the end, cut it lengthwise to create a small tassle.

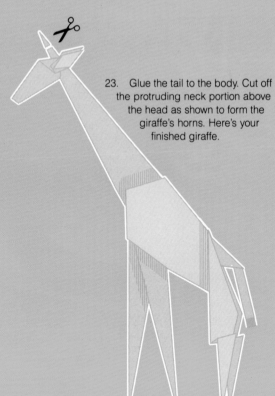

23. Glue the tail to the body. Cut off the protruding neck portion above the head as shown to form the giraffe's horns. Here's your finished giraffe.

With one leap, a kangaroo can cover a distance of 42 feet (13 metres), and reach a height of almost 10 feet (3 metres). And it makes absolutely no difference whether or not the kangaroo is carrying its offspring in its pouch. This unusual marsupial mammal, native to Australia, has front legs that seem too short, strong hind limbs, and a muscular tail. The best-known kangaroos are the red and the grey large kangaroos, both as tall as a human, weighing up to 220 pounds (100 kilograms). The red kangaroo lives primarily in the steppes, eats grass, and can be found all over the Australian continent. Only the male has a red coat; the fur of the female is a smoky blue. The grey kangaroo can be found mostly in the forests of eastern Australia. A kangaroo pack has about 12 members. All together, there are about 50 varieties of kangaroos. The smallest are the kangaroo rats, tree kangaroos, and rabbit kangaroos. Australian farmers are very concerned about the presence of the red kangaroo because it eats the grass that the farmer needs for his sheep. And sheep are an important part of the Australian economy. Competition has assumed dangerous proportions, especially since farmers have increased the available grassland.

Kangaroo

Body

When feeding, kangaroos sway on their short fore legs and strong tail while the longer hind legs swing forward.

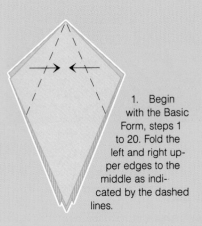

1. Begin with the Basic Form, steps 1 to 20. Fold the left and right upper edges to the middle as indicated by the dashed lines.

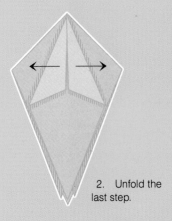

2. Unfold the last step.

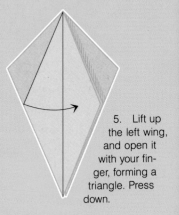

3. Lift up the right "wing," and open it with your finger, forming a triangle. Press down.

Kangaroos jump as though they had built-in springs. They push off with their strong hind legs and use the tail as a rudder to steer.

When escaping from danger, kangaroos may reach a speed of nearly 50 miles (80 kilometres) per hour.

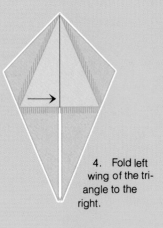

4. Fold left wing of the triangle to the right.

5. Lift up the left wing, and open it with your finger, forming a triangle. Press down.

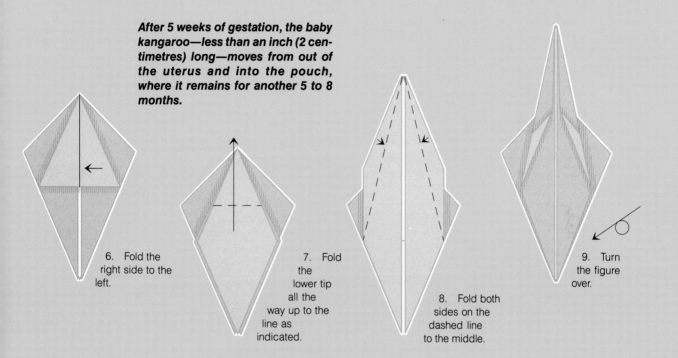

After 5 weeks of gestation, the baby kangaroo—less than an inch (2 centimetres) long—moves from out of the uterus and into the pouch, where it remains for another 5 to 8 months.

6. Fold the right side to the left.

7. Fold the lower tip all the way up to the line as indicated.

8. Fold both sides on the dashed line to the middle.

9. Turn the figure over.

A baby kangaroo in a pouch is called a "joey."

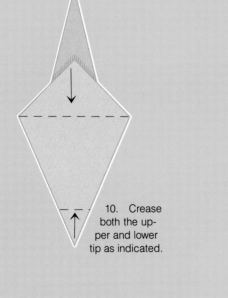

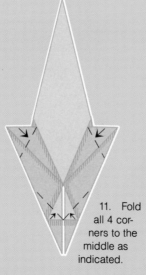

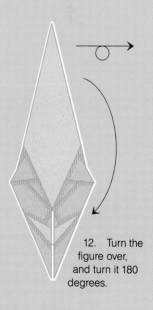

10. Crease both the upper and lower tip as indicated.

11. Fold all 4 corners to the middle as indicated.

12. Turn the figure over, and turn it 180 degrees.

63

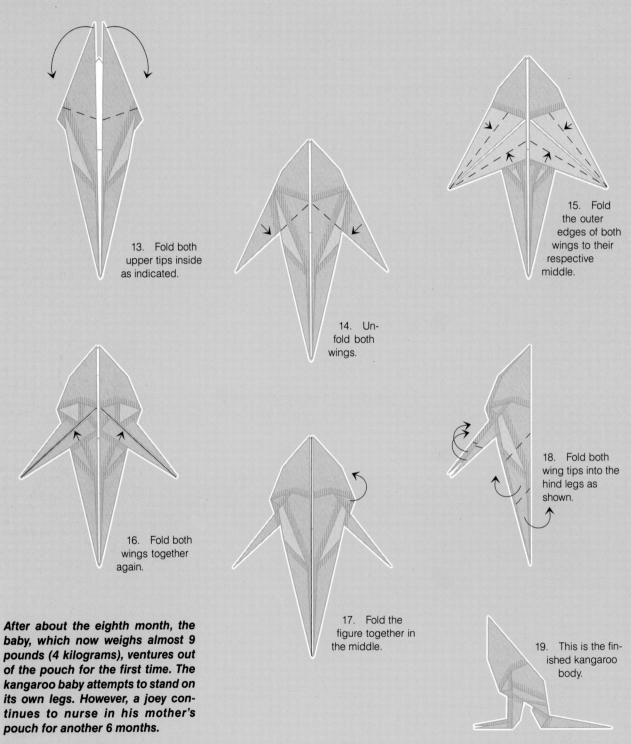

13. Fold both upper tips inside as indicated.

14. Unfold both wings.

15. Fold the outer edges of both wings to their respective middle.

16. Fold both wings together again.

17. Fold the figure together in the middle.

18. Fold both wing tips into the hind legs as shown.

19. This is the finished kangaroo body.

After about the eighth month, the baby, which now weighs almost 9 pounds (4 kilograms), ventures out of the pouch for the first time. The kangaroo baby attempts to stand on its own legs. However, a joey continues to nurse in his mother's pouch for another 6 months.

Head

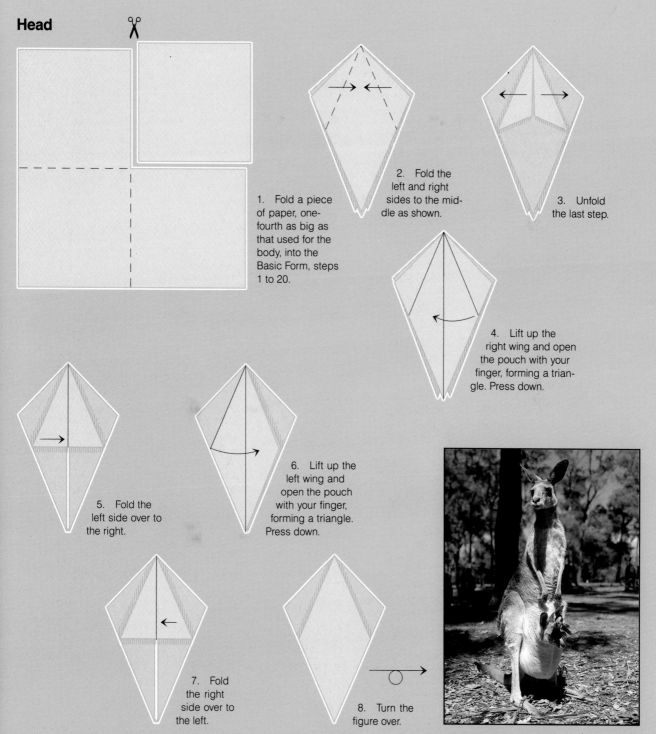

1. Fold a piece of paper, one-fourth as big as that used for the body, into the Basic Form, steps 1 to 20.

2. Fold the left and right sides to the middle as shown.

3. Unfold the last step.

4. Lift up the right wing and open the pouch with your finger, forming a triangle. Press down.

5. Fold the left side over to the right.

6. Lift up the left wing and open the pouch with your finger, forming a triangle. Press down.

7. Fold the right side over to the left.

8. Turn the figure over.

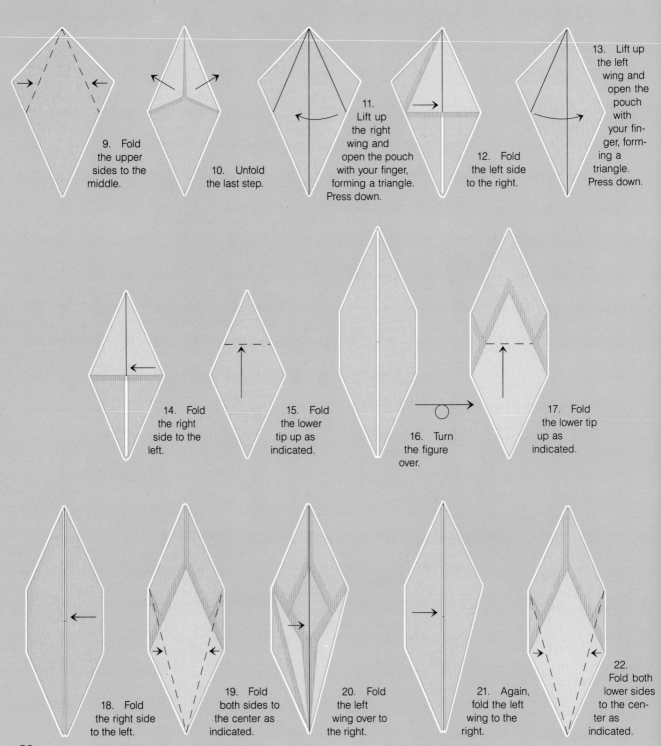

9. Fold the upper sides to the middle.

10. Unfold the last step.

11. Lift up the right wing and open the pouch with your finger, forming a triangle. Press down.

12. Fold the left side to the right.

13. Lift up the left wing and open the pouch with your finger, forming a triangle. Press down.

14. Fold the right side to the left.

15. Fold the lower tip up as indicated.

16. Turn the figure over.

17. Fold the lower tip up as indicated.

18. Fold the right side to the left.

19. Fold both sides to the center as indicated.

20. Fold the left wing over to the right.

21. Again, fold the left wing to the right.

22. Fold both lower sides to the center as indicated.

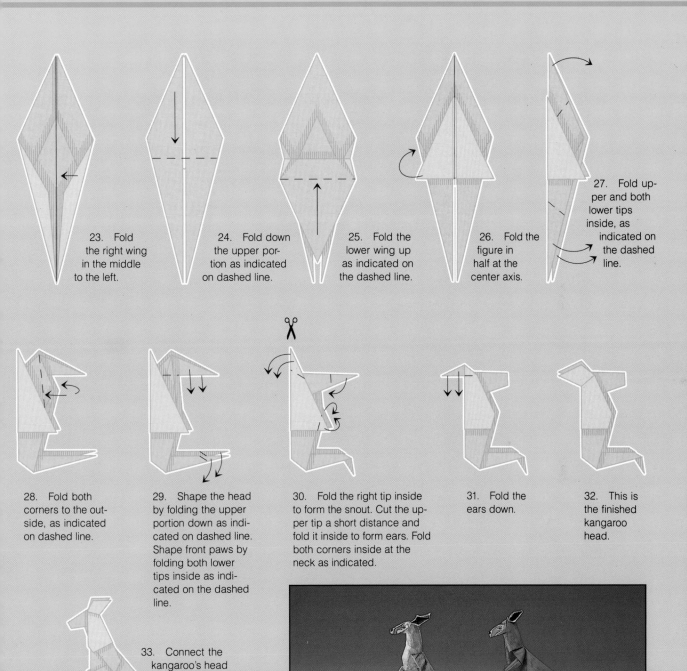

23. Fold the right wing in the middle to the left.

24. Fold down the upper portion as indicated on dashed line.

25. Fold the lower wing up as indicated on the dashed line.

26. Fold the figure in half at the center axis.

27. Fold upper and both lower tips inside, as indicated on the dashed line.

28. Fold both corners to the outside, as indicated on dashed line.

29. Shape the head by folding the upper portion down as indicated on dashed line. Shape front paws by folding both lower tips inside as indicated on the dashed line.

30. Fold the right tip inside to form the snout. Cut the upper tip a short distance and fold it inside to form ears. Fold both corners inside at the neck as indicated.

31. Fold the ears down.

32. This is the finished kangaroo head.

33. Connect the kangaroo's head and body, and glue them into place.

The deer family includes many different species. Except for the musk deer, all male members have antlers, which only vary in shape. A young stag has small antlers, which he sheds every spring. It takes about 100 days for new antlers to grow. The antlers increase every year until the stag reaches maturity and full strength, 9 to 12 years. In the fall, during the rutting season, when male deers' antlers are at their most impressive, stags vie for hinds with their mating calls reverberating through the forest. Using their antlers, stags engage in fierce fights during courtship. However, they seldom inflict serious injuries on each other. After 33 weeks, during May or June, the young are born. Male deer then establish their own herd, as do the female deer with their young. The fallow deer lives in mixed forests, parks with dense tree growth, and lower mountain regions. Its antlers are palm-shaped. The middle-European red deer and the North American white-tailed deer, as well as other species living in the northern hemisphere, have impressive antlers and a mane.

Deer

Hindquarters

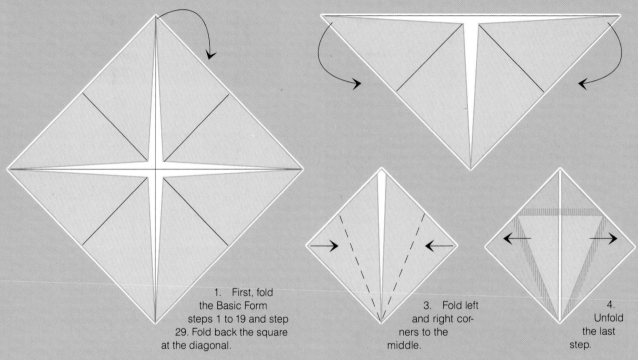

1. First, fold the Basic Form steps 1 to 19 and step 29. Fold back the square at the diagonal.

3. Fold left and right corners to the middle.

4. Unfold the last step.

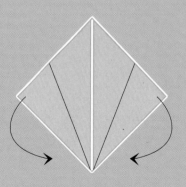

5. Fold both outer corners at the crease inside.

72

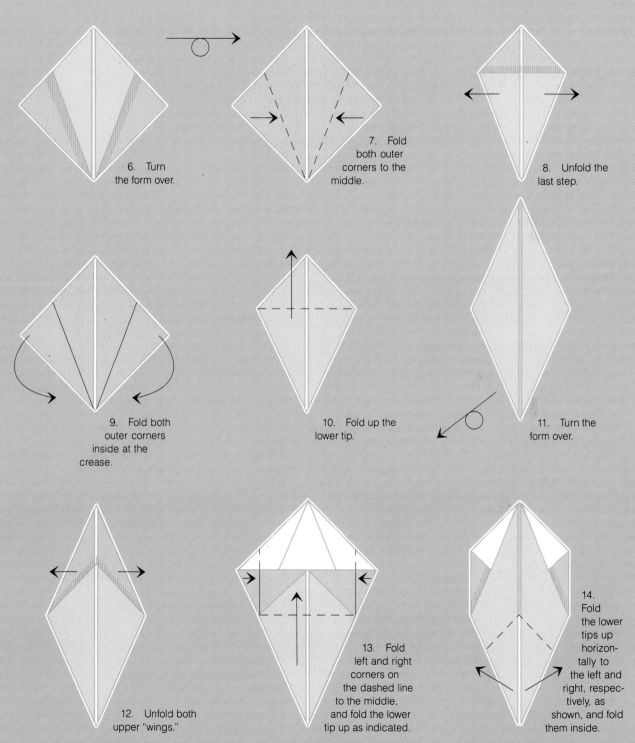

6. Turn the form over.

7. Fold both outer corners to the middle.

8. Unfold the last step.

9. Fold both outer corners inside at the crease.

10. Fold up the lower tip.

11. Turn the form over.

12. Unfold both upper "wings."

13. Fold left and right corners on the dashed line to the middle, and fold the lower tip up as indicated.

14. Fold the lower tips up horizontally to the left and right, respectively, as shown, and fold them inside.

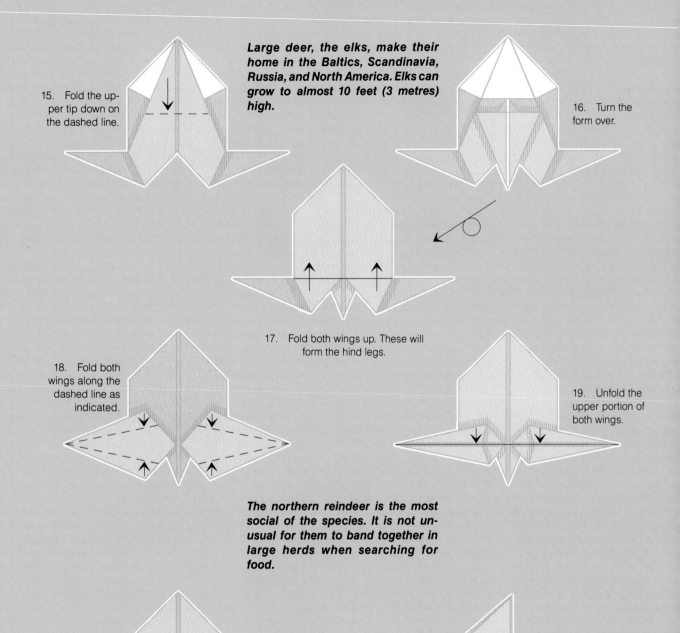

15. Fold the upper tip down on the dashed line.

Large deer, the elks, make their home in the Baltics, Scandinavia, Russia, and North America. Elks can grow to almost 10 feet (3 metres) high.

16. Turn the form over.

17. Fold both wings up. These will form the hind legs.

18. Fold both wings along the dashed line as indicated.

19. Unfold the upper portion of both wings.

The northern reindeer is the most social of the species. It is not unusual for them to band together in large herds when searching for food.

20. Fold back the figure at the middle.

21. Crease the tail and hind legs on the dashed line as indicated.

Front Portion

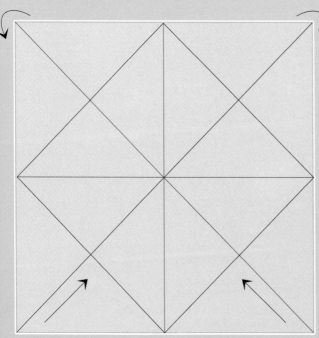

1. Start with the Basic Form steps 1 to 10 and steps 29 to 31. Fold the lower corners to the middle and the upper corners back to the middle, as indicated.

2. Fold the form back diagonally.

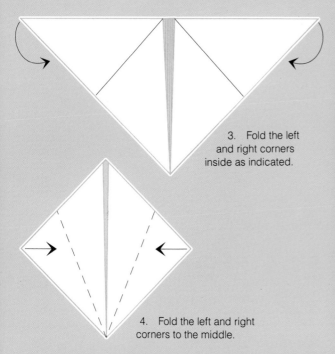

3. Fold the left and right corners inside as indicated.

4. Fold the left and right corners to the middle.

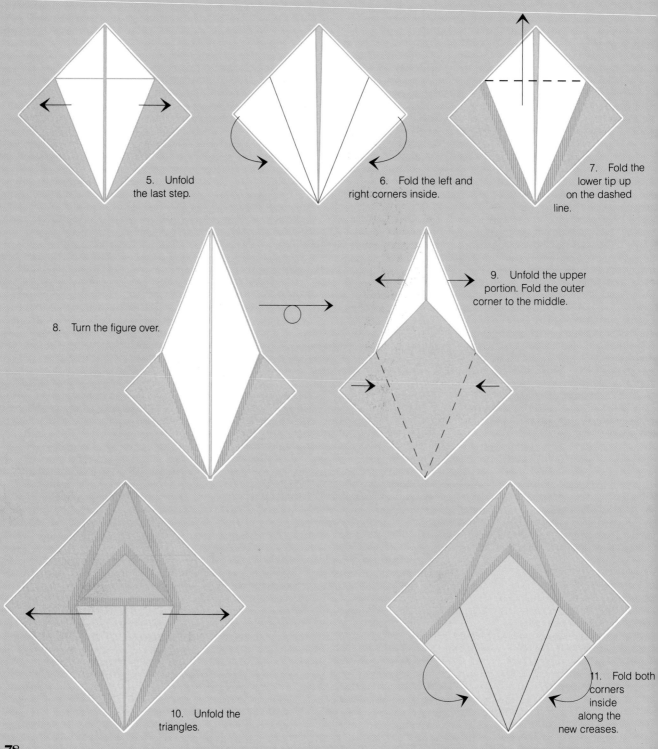

5. Unfold the last step.

6. Fold the left and right corners inside.

7. Fold the lower tip up on the dashed line.

8. Turn the figure over.

9. Unfold the upper portion. Fold the outer corner to the middle.

10. Unfold the triangles.

11. Fold both corners inside along the new creases.

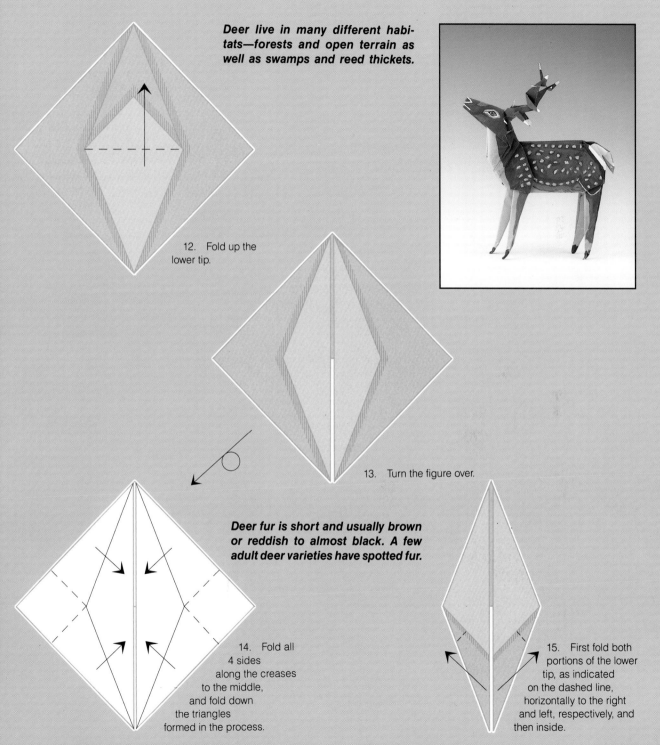

Deer live in many different habitats—forests and open terrain as well as swamps and reed thickets.

12. Fold up the lower tip.

13. Turn the figure over.

Deer fur is short and usually brown or reddish to almost black. A few adult deer varieties have spotted fur.

14. Fold all 4 sides along the creases to the middle, and fold down the triangles formed in the process.

15. First fold both portions of the lower tip, as indicated on the dashed line, horizontally to the right and left, respectively, and then inside.

79

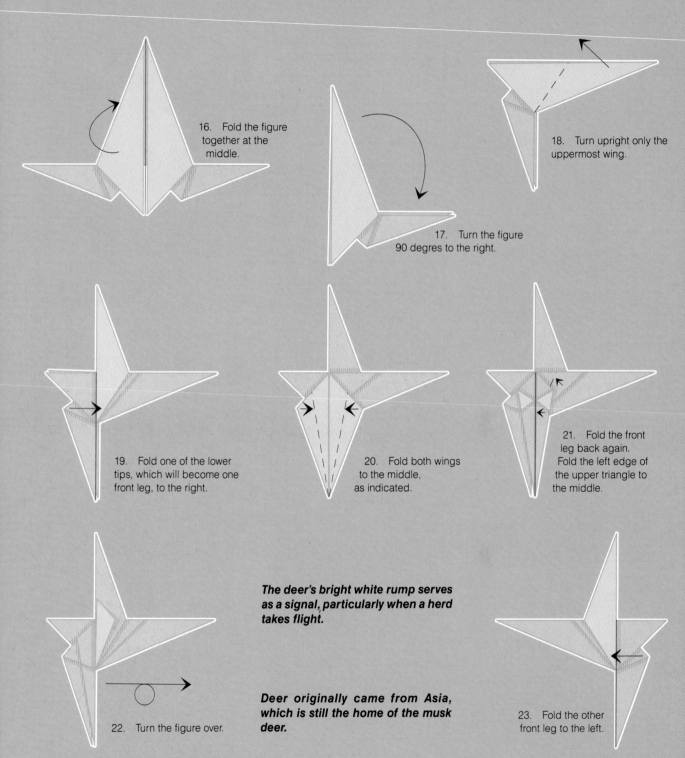

16. Fold the figure together at the middle.

17. Turn the figure 90 degrees to the right.

18. Turn upright only the uppermost wing.

19. Fold one of the lower tips, which will become one front leg, to the right.

20. Fold both wings to the middle, as indicated.

21. Fold the front leg back again. Fold the left edge of the upper triangle to the middle.

The deer's bright white rump serves as a signal, particularly when a herd takes flight.

22. Turn the figure over.

Deer originally came from Asia, which is still the home of the musk deer.

23. Fold the other front leg to the left.

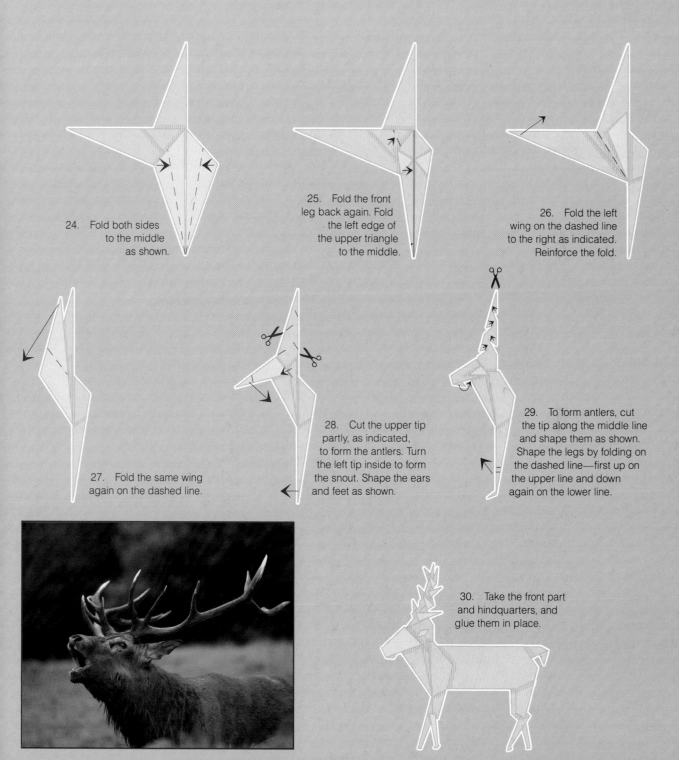

24. Fold both sides to the middle as shown.

25. Fold the front leg back again. Fold the left edge of the upper triangle to the middle.

26. Fold the left wing on the dashed line to the right as indicated. Reinforce the fold.

27. Fold the same wing again on the dashed line.

28. Cut the upper tip partly, as indicated, to form the antlers. Turn the left tip inside to form the snout. Shape the ears and feet as shown.

29. To form antlers, cut the tip along the middle line and shape them as shown. Shape the legs by folding on the dashed line—first up on the upper line and down again on the lower line.

30. Take the front part and hindquarters, and glue them in place.

Try to imagine, several million years ago, turtles crawling about the huge feet of dinosaurs. Although most turtle species were larger back then, they really have not changed. Turtles today still have a thick shell made from bone plates and horn that covers the whole body. When turtles confront danger, they pull the head, neck, tail, and legs inside the shell. Many turtle species have become extinct, and many hover on the brink of extinction. Today only 12 species, which include about 200 different types, still exist. From the very beginning, turtles lived in tropical and moderate regions of the globe, in both freshwater and salt water, and in varied habitats—forests, steppes, and deserts. Water and sea turtles eat dead animals. Land turtles, however, are herbivores. All turtles deposit their eggs in the ground, even freshwater turtles and sea turtles. The sun supplies the warmth necessary for the eggs to hatch.

Turtle

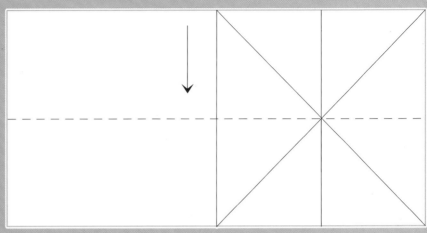

1. Begin by following the Basic Form steps 34 to 44. Fold the upper half down to the lower half.

2. Fold the right half along the creases to the middle.

European water and swamp turtles are shy and easily frightened. They love running streams, and after sun-down, they crawl onto land and be-come fairly active.

3. Fold the upper and lower corners along the dashed line as shown.

4. Unfold the last step.

Many children are particularly fond of turtles. However, two-thirds of all turtles kept as pets die within the first year of captivity, usually from lack of appropriate care.

5. Fold both corners inside along the creases.

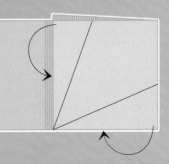

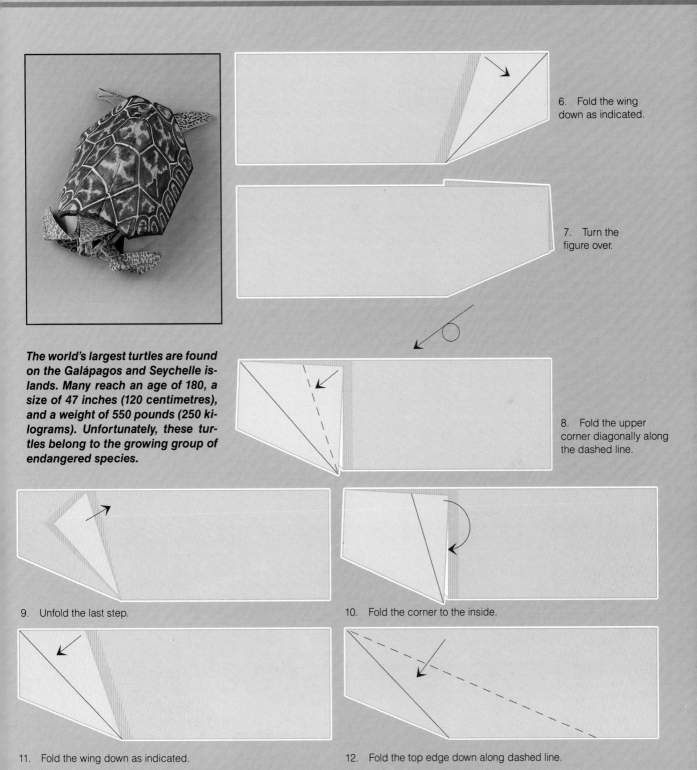

6. Fold the wing down as indicated.

7. Turn the figure over.

The world's largest turtles are found on the Galápagos and Seychelle islands. Many reach an age of 180, a size of 47 inches (120 centimetres), and a weight of 550 pounds (250 kilograms). Unfortunately, these turtles belong to the growing group of endangered species.

8. Fold the upper corner diagonally along the dashed line.

9. Unfold the last step.

10. Fold the corner to the inside.

11. Fold the wing down as indicated.

12. Fold the top edge down along dashed line.

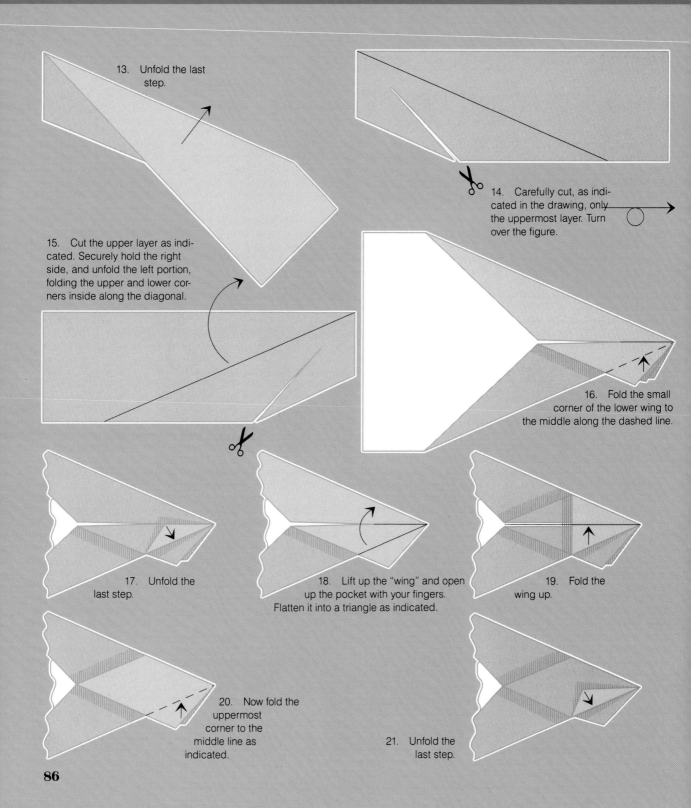

13. Unfold the last step.

14. Carefully cut, as indicated in the drawing, only the uppermost layer. Turn over the figure.

15. Cut the upper layer as indicated. Securely hold the right side, and unfold the left portion, folding the upper and lower corners inside along the diagonal.

16. Fold the small corner of the lower wing to the middle along the dashed line.

17. Unfold the last step.

18. Lift up the "wing" and open up the pocket with your fingers. Flatten it into a triangle as indicated.

19. Fold the wing up.

20. Now fold the uppermost corner to the middle line as indicated.

21. Unfold the last step.

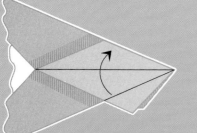

22. Lift up the wing and the open pocket. Flatten it into a triangle.

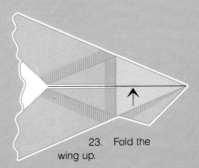

23. Fold the wing up.

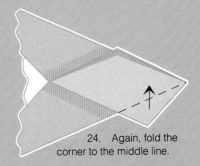

24. Again, fold the corner to the middle line.

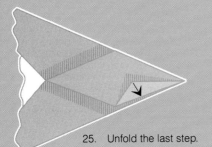

25. Unfold the last step.

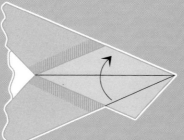

26. Lift up the wing and the open pocket. Flatten it into a triangle as indicated.

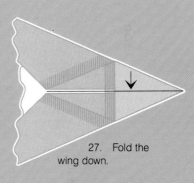

27. Fold the wing down.

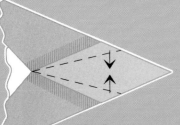

28. Fold the upper and lower edges to the middle along the dashed line.

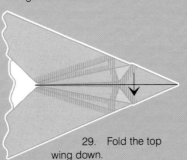

29. Fold the top wing down.

The most resilient turtles are the Greek land turtles. They often grow much older than humans.

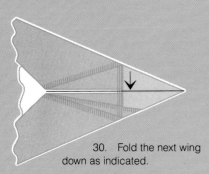

30. Fold the next wing down as indicated.

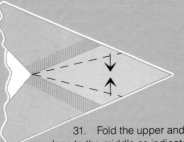

31. Fold the upper and lower edges to the middle as indicated.

87

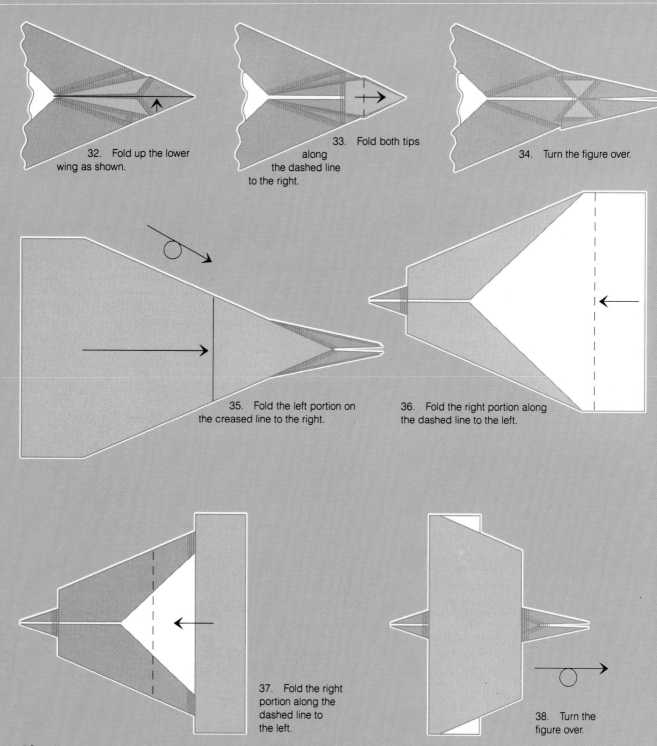

32. Fold up the lower wing as shown.

33. Fold both tips along the dashed line to the right.

34. Turn the figure over.

35. Fold the left portion on the creased line to the right.

36. Fold the right portion along the dashed line to the left.

37. Fold the right portion along the dashed line to the left.

38. Turn the figure over.

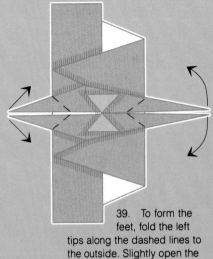

Land turtles are more docile than sea turtles. Sea turtles like to bite.

39. To form the feet, fold the left tips along the dashed lines to the outside. Slightly open the right tips, and fold them inside along the dashed lines.

40. Fold the upper and lower squares along the dashed line, and slide them slightly into each other.

41. Fold all four corners inside as shown.

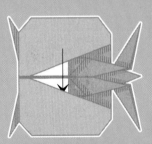

42. Continue sliding the body together as shown.

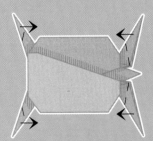

43. Fold both hind legs toward the body and the front feet to the outside.

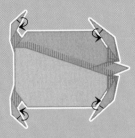

44. Fold the tips of the feet inside.

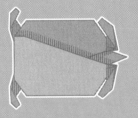

45. Turn the figure 90 degrees.

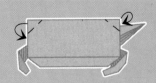

46. Fold the corners at the tip of the tail and head plates inside.

Gracefully moving on stilt-like legs, the flamingo in his appearance reminds us of the giraffe. The flamingo's neck and legs seem out of proportion to his body, and they are longer than those of most other birds. Shallow lakes and lagoons are their turf; there they find abundant food—aquatic plants and animals. Standing in large numbers in brackish water, flamingos may feed continuously for as long as 15 hours a day. During this time, about 92 quarts (350 litres) of water flow through the beak that is specially shaped like a filter, to trap thousands of tiny crabs. These crabs give flamingo feathers their salmon pink color. The still snow-white young look much more like little goose chicks. The downy young leave the nest within three days. Only one egg is incubated at a time, a job that both male and female flamingos share. Three-day-old flamingos can walk and immediately join the large flock. Their parents readily distinguish their offspring from the flock, and feed them by regurgitating food. Although colonies of 800,000 flamingos live on Lake Nakuru in Kenya, flamingos are considered endangered species almost everywhere. They inhabit Africa, Madagascar, southern Europe, France (La Camargue), western India, the Caribbean, the Galápagos Islands, and South America.

Adult Flamingo

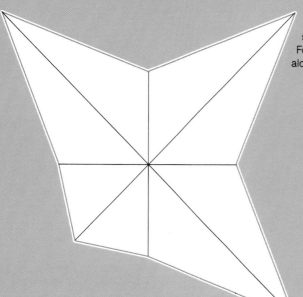

1. Start with the Basic Form, steps 1 to 25. Fold the paper together along existing creases.

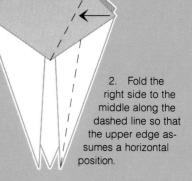

2. Fold the right side to the middle along the dashed line so that the upper edge assumes a horizontal position.

3. Fold the left side just as you did the right side. Unfold the last step.

Flamingos always fly even small distances in flocks, never singly.

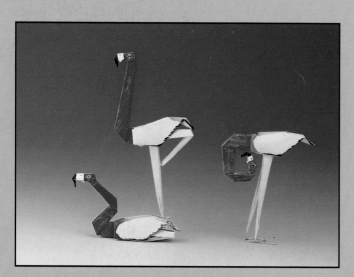

4. Also, unfold the left side as shown.

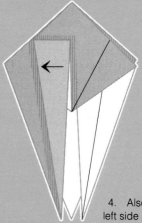

94

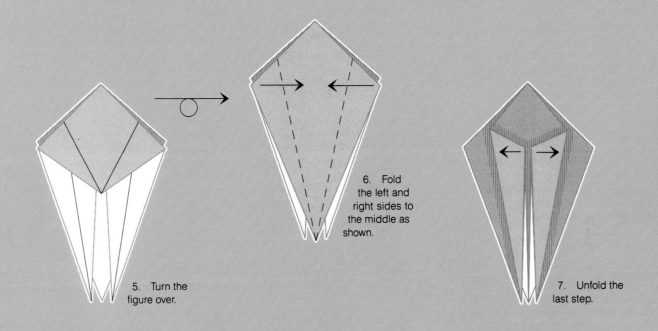

6. Fold the left and right sides to the middle as shown.

5. Turn the figure over.

7. Unfold the last step.

Flamingos have a long, graceful neck, and long, thin legs. They can grow as tall as 6 feet (190 cm).

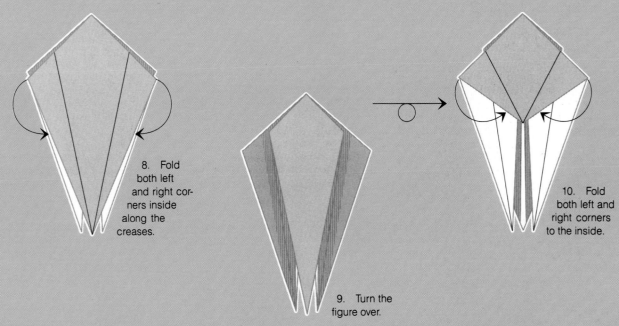

8. Fold both left and right corners inside along the creases.

10. Fold both left and right corners to the inside.

9. Turn the figure over.

The flamingo's "hooked" beak is Mother Nature's invention for filtering nourishment from sea water.

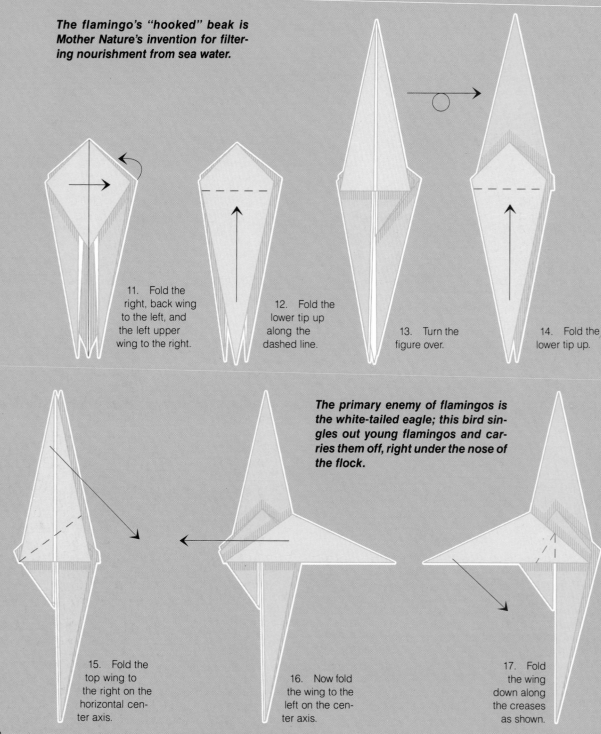

11. Fold the right, back wing to the left, and the left upper wing to the right.

12. Fold the lower tip up along the dashed line.

13. Turn the figure over.

14. Fold the lower tip up.

The primary enemy of flamingos is the white-tailed eagle; this bird singles out young flamingos and carries them off, right under the nose of the flock.

15. Fold the top wing to the right on the horizontal center axis.

16. Now fold the wing to the left on the center axis.

17. Fold the wing down along the creases as shown.

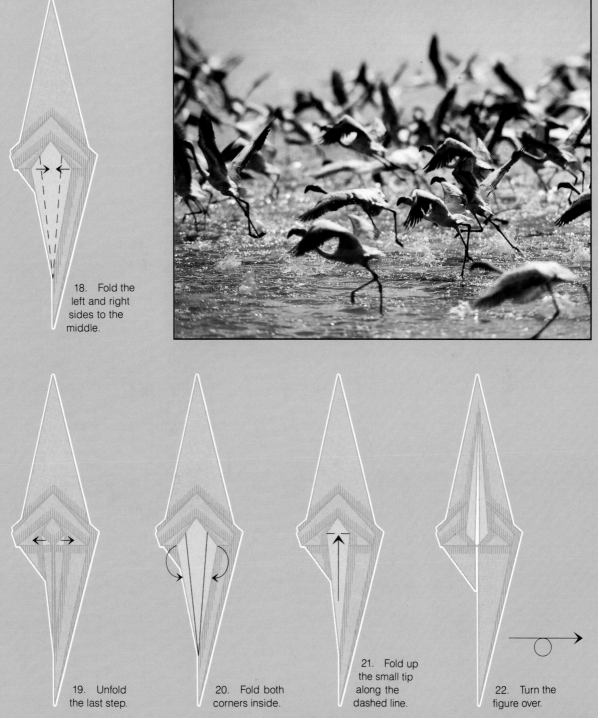

18. Fold the left and right sides to the middle.

19. Unfold the last step.

20. Fold both corners inside.

21. Fold up the small tip along the dashed line.

22. Turn the figure over.

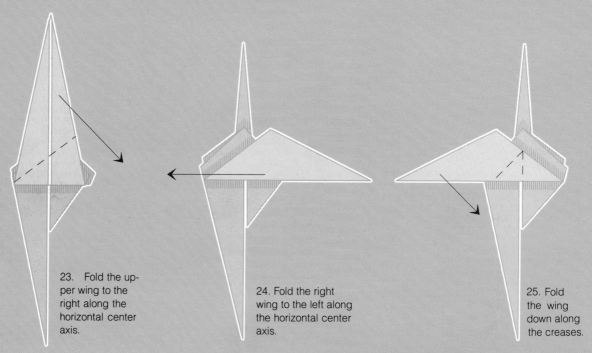

23. Fold the up-per wing to the right along the horizontal center axis.

24. Fold the right wing to the left along the horizontal center axis.

25. Fold the wing down along the creases.

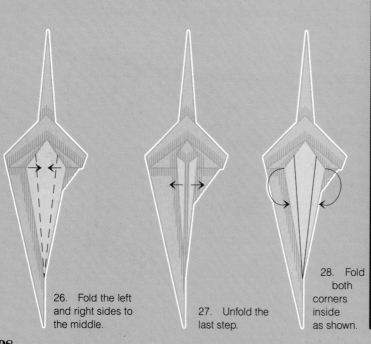

26. Fold the left and right sides to the middle.

27. Unfold the last step.

28. Fold both corners inside as shown.

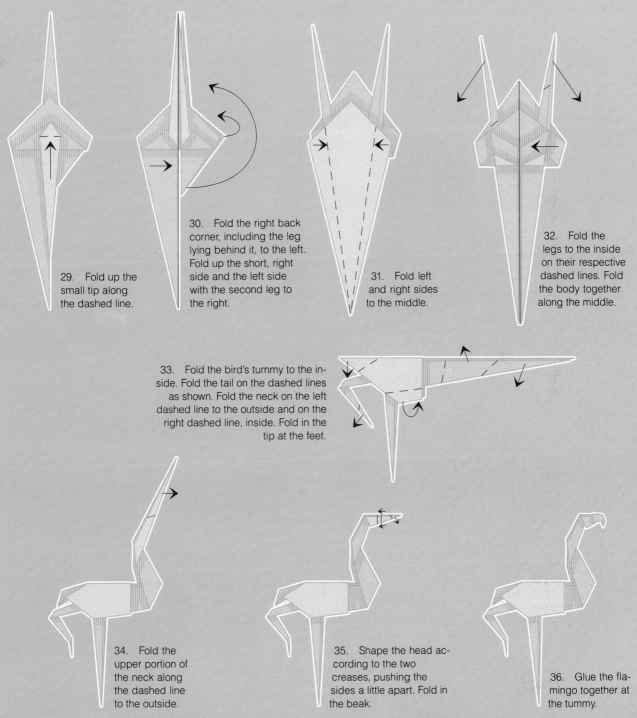

29. Fold up the small tip along the dashed line.

30. Fold the right back corner, including the leg lying behind it, to the left. Fold up the short, right side and the left side with the second leg to the right.

31. Fold left and right sides to the middle.

32. Fold the legs to the inside on their respective dashed lines. Fold the body together along the middle.

33. Fold the bird's tummy to the inside. Fold the tail on the dashed lines as shown. Fold the neck on the left dashed line to the outside and on the right dashed line, inside. Fold in the tip at the feet.

34. Fold the upper portion of the neck along the dashed line to the outside.

35. Shape the head according to the two creases, pushing the sides a little apart. Fold in the beak.

36. Glue the flamingo together at the tummy.

Baby Flamingo

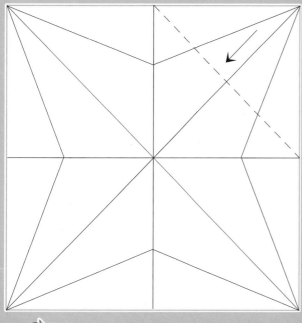

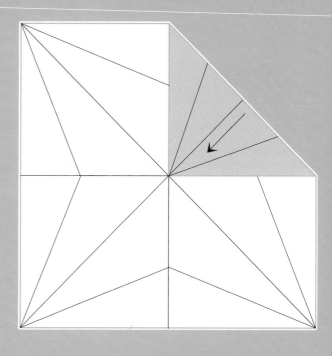

1. Start by folding the Basic Form steps 1 to 21. Fold the upper right corner to the middle.

2. Fold the paper together diagonally as shown.

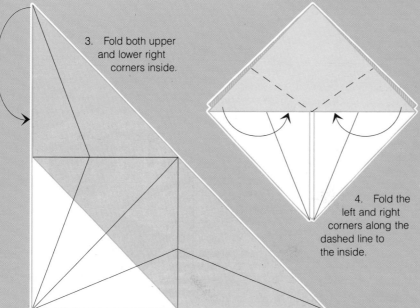

3. Fold both upper and lower right corners inside.

4. Fold the left and right corners along the dashed line to the inside.

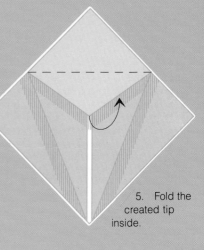

5. Fold the created tip inside.

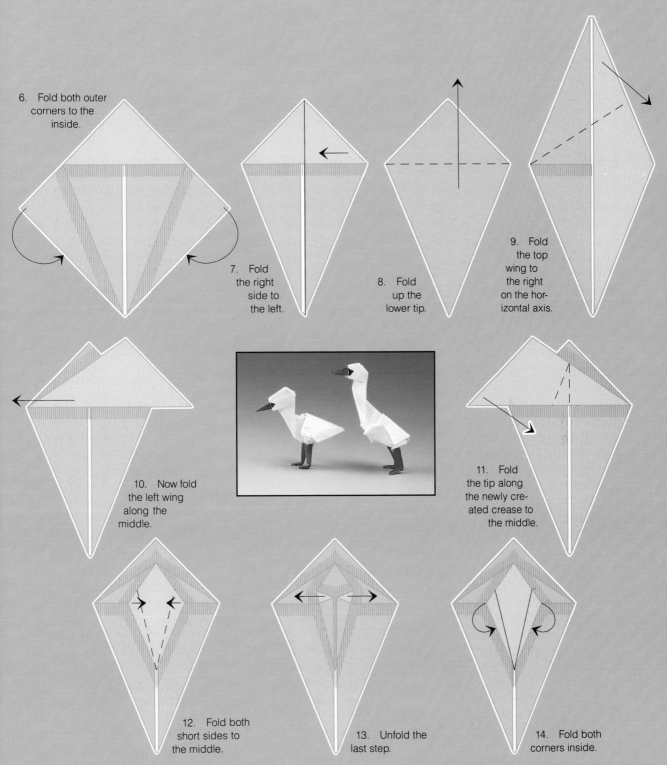

6. Fold both outer corners to the inside.

7. Fold the right side to the left.

8. Fold up the lower tip.

9. Fold the top wing to the right on the horizontal axis.

10. Now fold the left wing along the middle.

11. Fold the tip along the newly created crease to the middle.

12. Fold both short sides to the middle.

13. Unfold the last step.

14. Fold both corners inside.

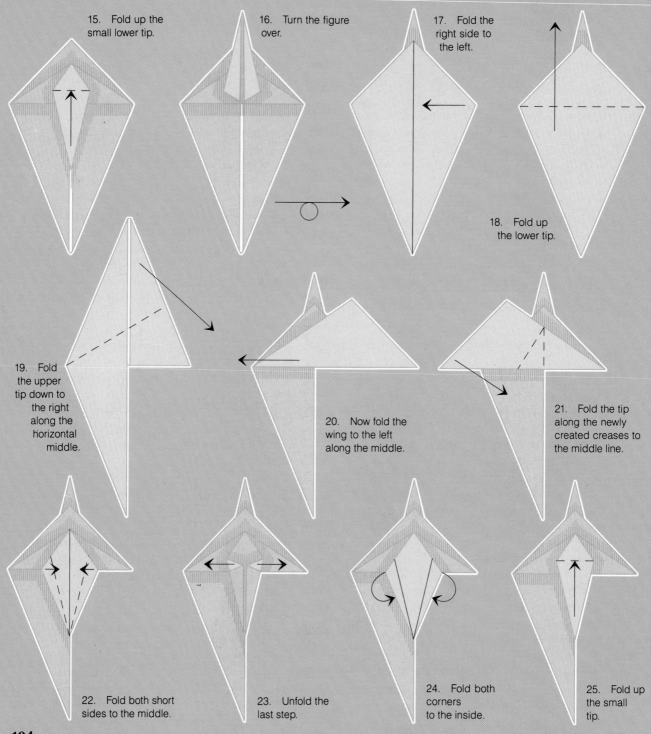

15. Fold up the small lower tip.

16. Turn the figure over.

17. Fold the right side to the left.

18. Fold up the lower tip.

19. Fold the upper tip down to the right along the horizontal middle.

20. Now fold the wing to the left along the middle.

21. Fold the tip along the newly created creases to the middle line.

22. Fold both short sides to the middle.

23. Unfold the last step.

24. Fold both corners to the inside.

25. Fold up the small tip.

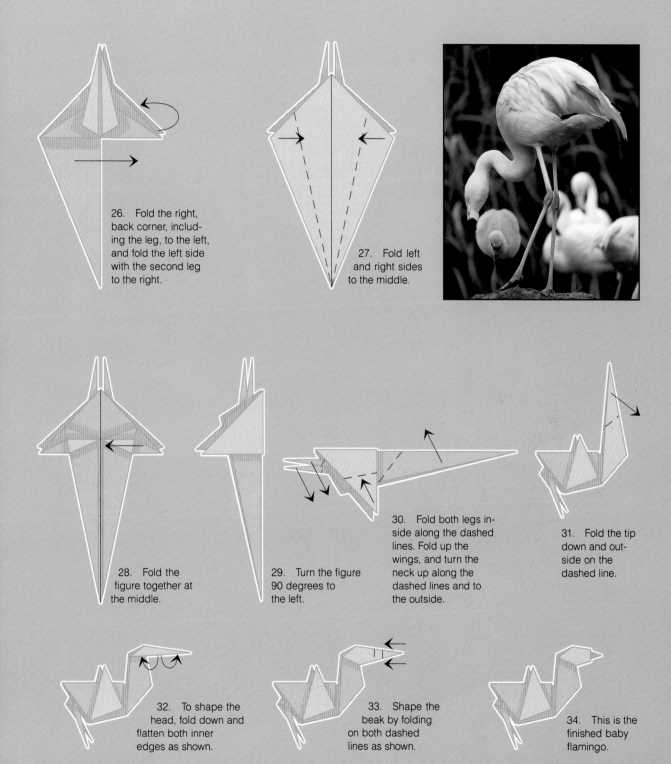

26. Fold the right, back corner, including the leg, to the left, and fold the left side with the second leg to the right.

27. Fold left and right sides to the middle.

28. Fold the figure together at the middle.

29. Turn the figure 90 degrees to the left.

30. Fold both legs inside along the dashed lines. Fold up the wings, and turn the neck up along the dashed lines and to the outside.

31. Fold the tip down and outside on the dashed line.

32. To shape the head, fold down and flatten both inner edges as shown.

33. Shape the beak by folding on both dashed lines as shown.

34. This is the finished baby flamingo.

The condor, a bird of prey, belongs to the family of New World vultures. He is at home in the Andes, from Venezuela to Colombia, all the way to the Strait of Magellan. The most characteristic feature for all birds of prey is the hook-shaped upper beak. Condors also have strong legs with long, short claws, and their gigantic wings may extend to over 10 feet (3 metres). Both the Andean condor and the smaller condor from California have superior flying skills. They live primarily on animal carcasses and only occasionally attack unprotected, helpless young mammals. These New World vultures are rather old, according to the evidence of fossil remains. They inhabited the earth as long as 40 to 50 million years ago. Apparently, they were also once present in the Old World. The California condor, more than the Andes condor, is close to extinction. Sadly, this majestic bird is a prime target for hunters. Also, chemical fertilizers used by farmers and growers have endangered it. Since the South American condor lives primarily in high elevations that are sparsely populated, his chances for survival are much better than those of the California variety.

Condor

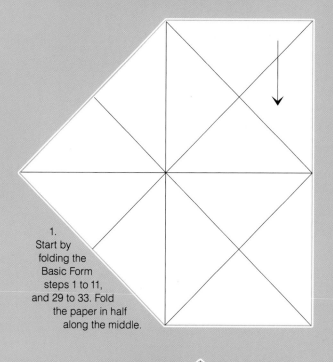

1.
Start by
folding the
Basic Form
steps 1 to 11,
and 29 to 33. Fold
the paper in half
along the middle.

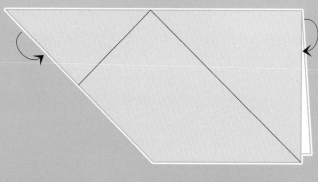

3. Fold the left cor-
ner to the middle line.

2. Fold the corners
along the creases to
the inside.

4. Fold the right
"wing" along the
dashed line to
the left.

5. Turn the
figure over.

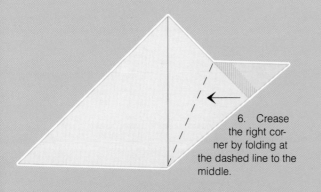

6. Crease the right corner by folding at the dashed line to the middle.

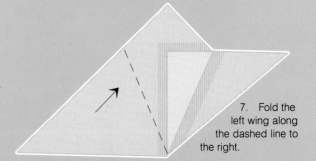

7. Fold the left wing along the dashed line to the right.

The Andean condor can grow to a height of about 51 inches (1.3 metres) and a weight of more than 22 pounds (10 kilograms).

8. This is how the figure should look.

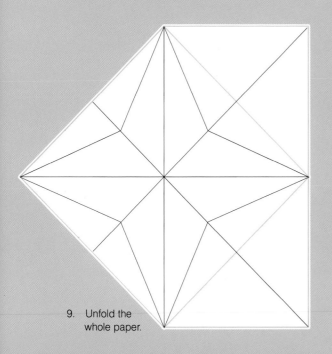

9. Unfold the whole paper.

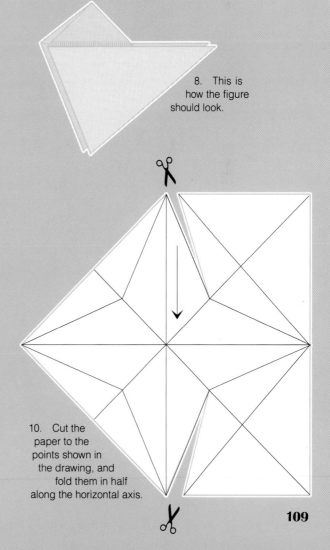

10. Cut the paper to the points shown in the drawing, and fold them in half along the horizontal axis.

109

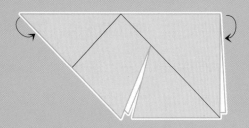

11. Fold the left and right corners to the inside along existing creases.

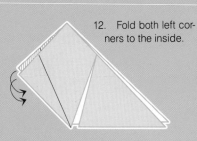

12. Fold both left corners to the inside.

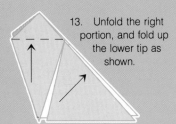

13. Unfold the right portion, and fold up the lower tip as shown.

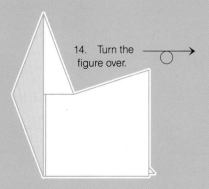

14. Turn the figure over.

15. Unfold the left portion, and fold up the lower tip.

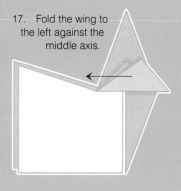

16. Fold the uppermost tip to the right against the horizontal axis along the dashed line.

People visiting zoos love to watch condors. In captivity condors often live to nearly 50 years old. However, it is hard to tell whether condors would reach such a ripe old age in the wild.

Sailing through the air, condors roam their territory daily.

17. Fold the wing to the left against the middle axis.

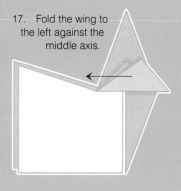

18. Fold down the wing in the newly created creases.

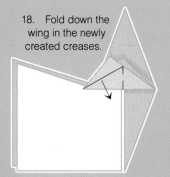

19. Fold the left and right sides to the middle axis.

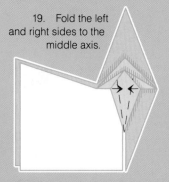

20. Unfold the last step.

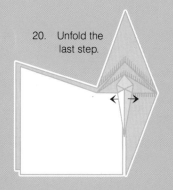

21. Fold both corners inside along the creases.

22. Fold up the small tip.

23. Turn the figure over.

24. Fold the left wing to the right on the dashed line to the horizontal axis.

25. Fold the wing to the left to the center axis.

26. Fold down the wing along the newly created creases.

27. Fold right and left sides to the middle as shown.

28. Unfold the last step.

29. Fold both corners along the newly created creases to the inside.

30. Fold up the small tip.

31. Fold the left side to the right and the half of the body below to the left.

32. Now fold back and up the newly un-folded wing as shown.

33. Fold the left and right lower cor-ners along the dashed line to the middle.

34. Unfold the last step.

35. Cut off both corners as shown. Cut out wings and tail along the exist-ing creases and dashed lines according to the drawing in step 34. Turn the figure around 180 degrees.

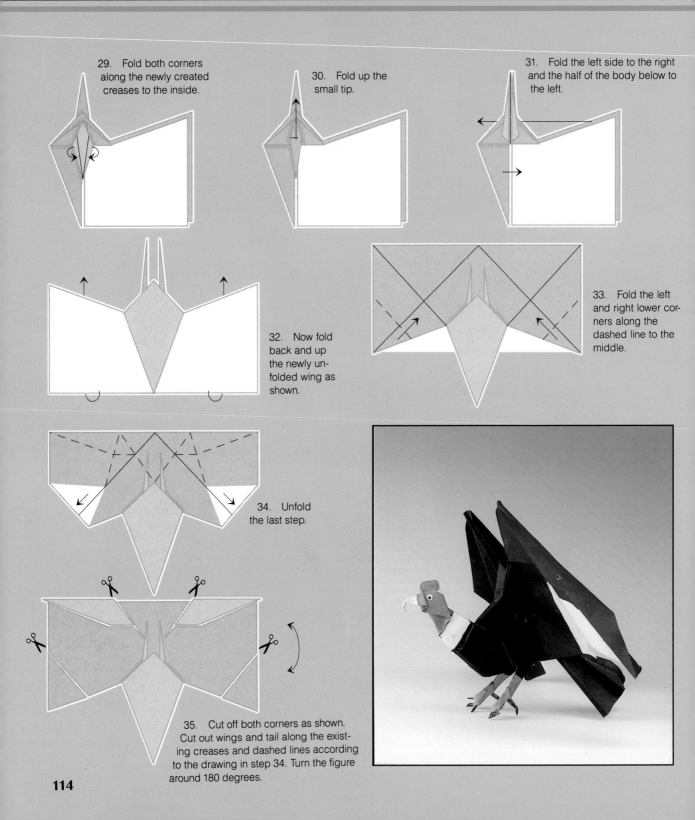

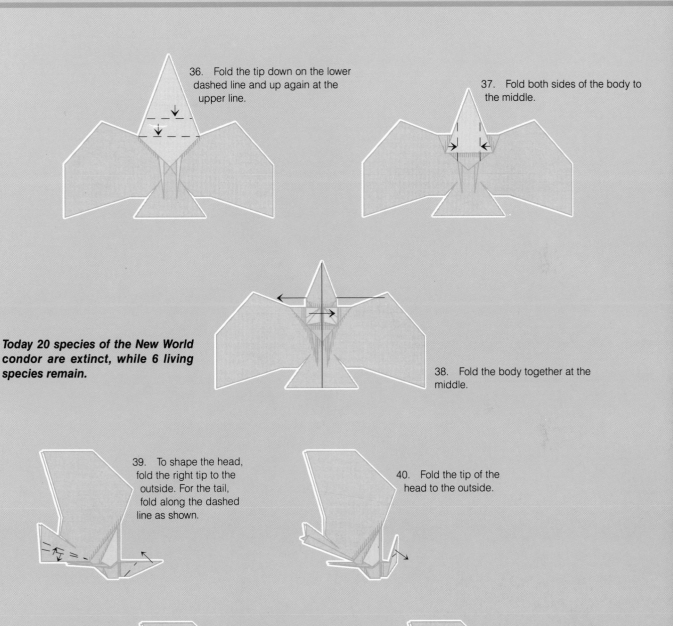

36. Fold the tip down on the lower dashed line and up again at the upper line.

37. Fold both sides of the body to the middle.

Today 20 species of the New World condor are extinct, while 6 living species remain.

38. Fold the body together at the middle.

39. To shape the head, fold the right tip to the outside. For the tail, fold along the dashed line as shown.

40. Fold the tip of the head to the outside.

41. Fold the feet down and inside. Form a beak by folding twice on the dashed line. Cut off the tip of the tail.

42. Glue the body together and round out the wings to finish your condor. Add some fancy claw feet, if you wish.

The toucan may be easily recognized by a huge beak, which in some of the nearly 40 species can be almost as large as the bird's whole body. It is uncertain why these birds need such a powerful tool, since they primarily eat tropical fruits. However, toucans will not reject a small insect or bird, since crunching them is no problem. Also, toucans rarely use the beak as a weapon. Toucans are native to South American tropical forests, primarily around the Amazon. They belong to the woodpecker family; they are 20 to 24 inches (50 to 60 centimetres) tall and often display colorful feathers. Brilliantly blue, green, and multicolored, smaller toucans are found in mountain forests ranging from southern Mexico to Argentina. They live in small flocks at various elevations, and, depending on the time of year, they feed on available fruits. Toucans sleep in hollow trees and fold themselves together, not unlike tropical flowers. The toucan turns her powerful beak so that it rests in the middle of her back and is completely covered with tail feathers; the tip of the tail touches the shoulders. The bird, in this position, looks like a flower growing between tree leaves.

Toucan

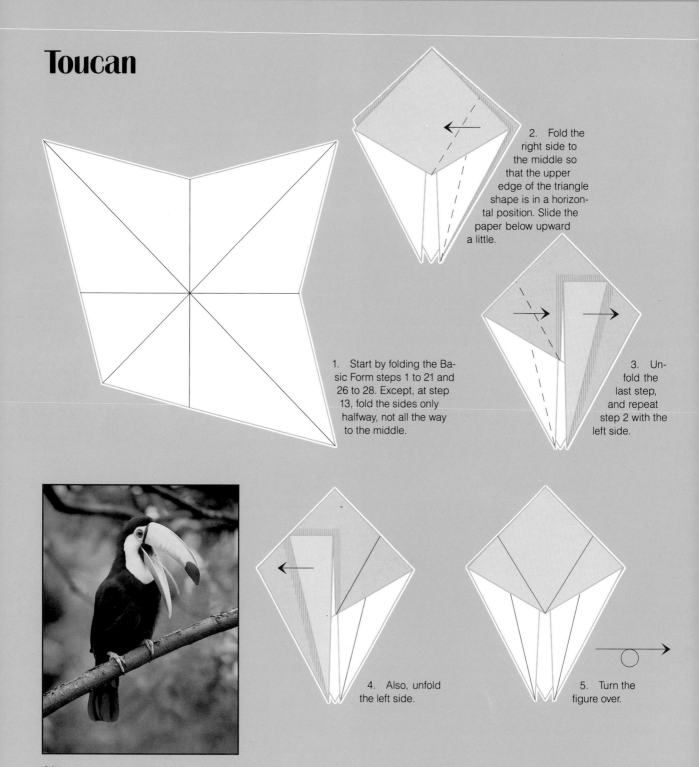

2. Fold the right side to the middle so that the upper edge of the triangle shape is in a horizontal position. Slide the paper below upward a little.

1. Start by folding the Basic Form steps 1 to 21 and 26 to 28. Except, at step 13, fold the sides only halfway, not all the way to the middle.

3. Unfold the last step, and repeat step 2 with the left side.

4. Also, unfold the left side.

5. Turn the figure over.

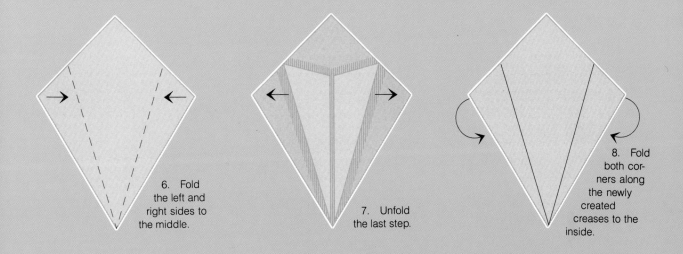

6. Fold the left and right sides to the middle.

7. Unfold the last step.

8. Fold both corners along the newly created creases to the inside.

The toucan is the clown of the jungle. With his large beak, he picks berries, throws them into the air, and catches the berries as they come down.

The toucan's most conspicuous characteristic is an often multicolored beak. Some have speculated that males use this huge beak to entice females during the mating season.

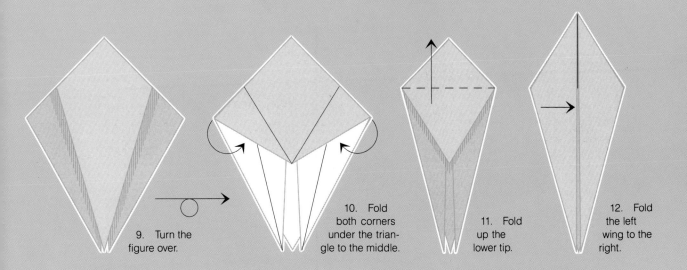

9. Turn the figure over.

10. Fold both corners under the triangle to the middle.

11. Fold up the lower tip.

12. Fold the left wing to the right.

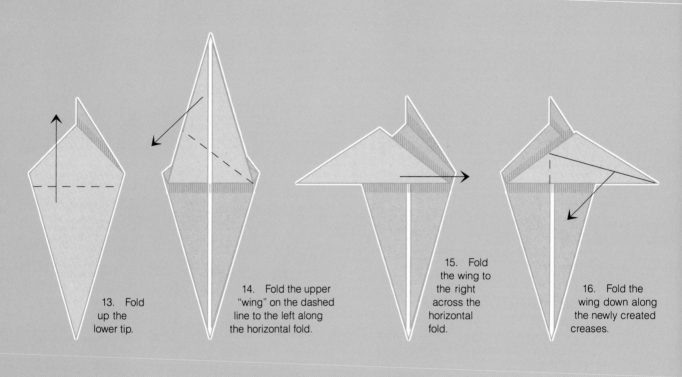

13. Fold up the lower tip.

14. Fold the upper "wing" on the dashed line to the left along the horizontal fold.

15. Fold the wing to the right across the horizontal fold.

16. Fold the wing down along the newly created creases.

The toucan rarely covers great distances in flight. Rather, he moves from one treetop to another by jumping from branch to branch.

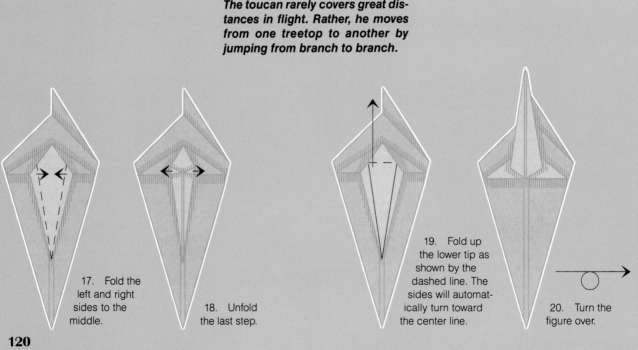

17. Fold the left and right sides to the middle.

18. Unfold the last step.

19. Fold up the lower tip as shown by the dashed line. The sides will automatically turn toward the center line.

20. Turn the figure over.

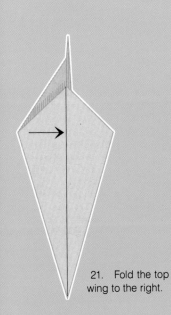

21. Fold the top wing to the right.

The Tupi Indians call this bird toco, a name adopted by explorers centuries ago, which has become toucan. In German, the bird is also called the pepper eater.

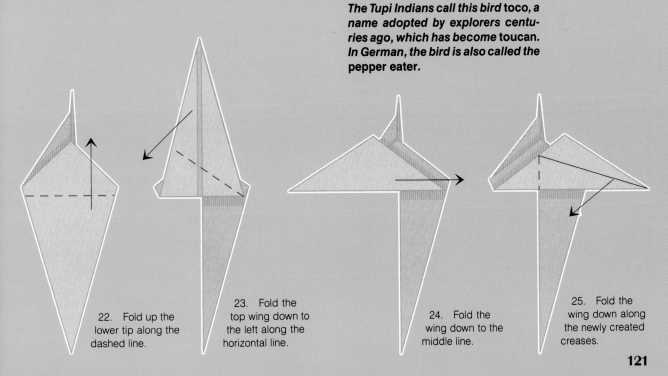

22. Fold up the lower tip along the dashed line.

23. Fold the top wing down to the left along the horizontal line.

24. Fold the wing down to the middle line.

25. Fold the wing down along the newly created creases.

121

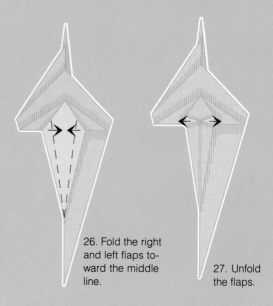

26. Fold the right and left flaps toward the middle line.

27. Unfold the flaps.

The loud, croaking sound of the toucan can be heard in the jungle throughout the day.

When in flight, the toucan's heavy beak always points down, creating a rather unbalanced situation.

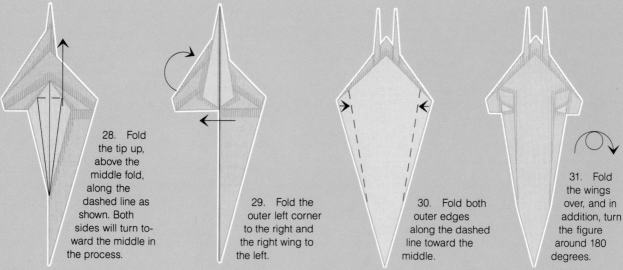

28. Fold the tip up, above the middle fold, along the dashed line as shown. Both sides will turn toward the middle in the process.

29. Fold the outer left corner to the right and the right wing to the left.

30. Fold both outer edges along the dashed line toward the middle.

31. Fold the wings over, and in addition, turn the figure around 180 degrees.

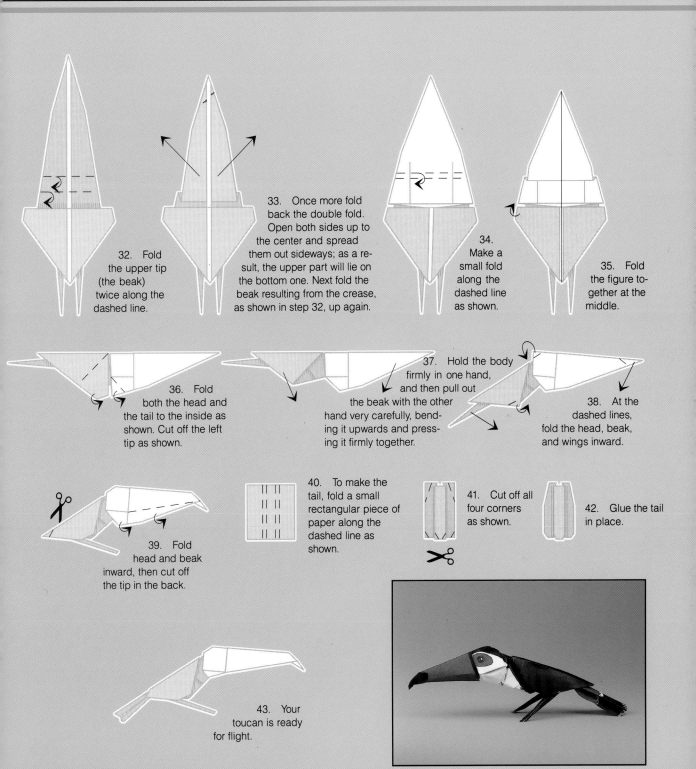

32. Fold the upper tip (the beak) twice along the dashed line.

33. Once more fold back the double fold. Open both sides up to the center and spread them out sideways; as a result, the upper part will lie on the bottom one. Next fold the beak resulting from the crease, as shown in step 32, up again.

34. Make a small fold along the dashed line as shown.

35. Fold the figure together at the middle.

36. Fold both the head and the tail to the inside as shown. Cut off the left tip as shown.

37. Hold the body firmly in one hand, and then pull out the beak with the other hand very carefully, bending it upwards and pressing it firmly together.

38. At the dashed lines, fold the head, beak, and wings inward.

39. Fold head and beak inward, then cut off the tip in the back.

40. To make the tail, fold a small rectangular piece of paper along the dashed line as shown.

41. Cut off all four corners as shown.

42. Glue the tail in place.

43. Your toucan is ready for flight.

Tarantulas belong to the large spider family, which has more than 30,000 members. This family of wolf spiders has about 1,500 members. Wolf spiders do not build webs; instead, they stalk their prey like a predator. The most notorious is the Apulian tarantula, which grows to about 1½ inches (3 centimetres) and lives in the Mediterranean region. During the day the Apulian hides in tunnels in the earth, which are often as deep as 12 inches (30 centimetres), and hunts for insects at night. His bite is very painful, but contrary to popular opinion, it is not dangerous to humans. Female wolf spiders make excellent parents. She carries eggs on her back in a specially constructed cocoon, and when the young hatch, she carries them on her back until they are fully grown. Spiders characteristically have a narrow waist-like indentation, which divides the body into front and hindquarters, as well as a spinning wart. Both front legs are used to grab and hold, while the back legs are used for locomotion. The secretion from the spinning wart is used to make the thread, a kind of security rope, used to lower the tarantula from trees and branches as well as from other spiders' webs and traps.

Tarantula

All spiders are predators. They use threads to tie up their victims, build webs, or spin individual threads—sometimes covered with a sticky substance—over which insects stumble.

The large ¾-inch (2-centimetre) garden, or cross, spider with a greyish body, triangular or cross-shaped ornament on the back, and very hairy legs looks more dangerous than it really is.

1. Start by folding the Basic Form steps 1 to 21.

2. Cut paper according to the drawing, and fold all 4 corners to their respective middle line.

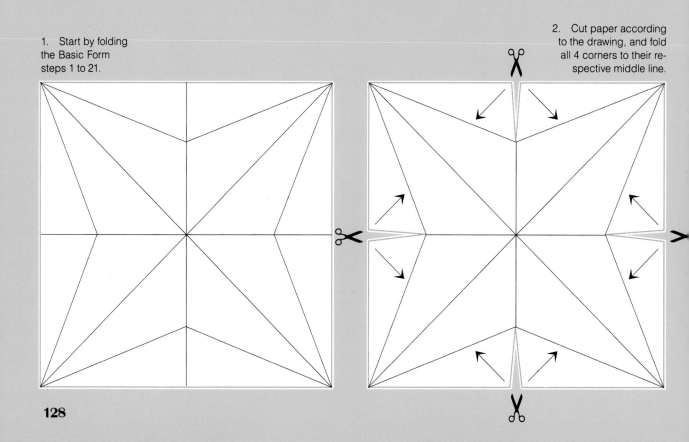

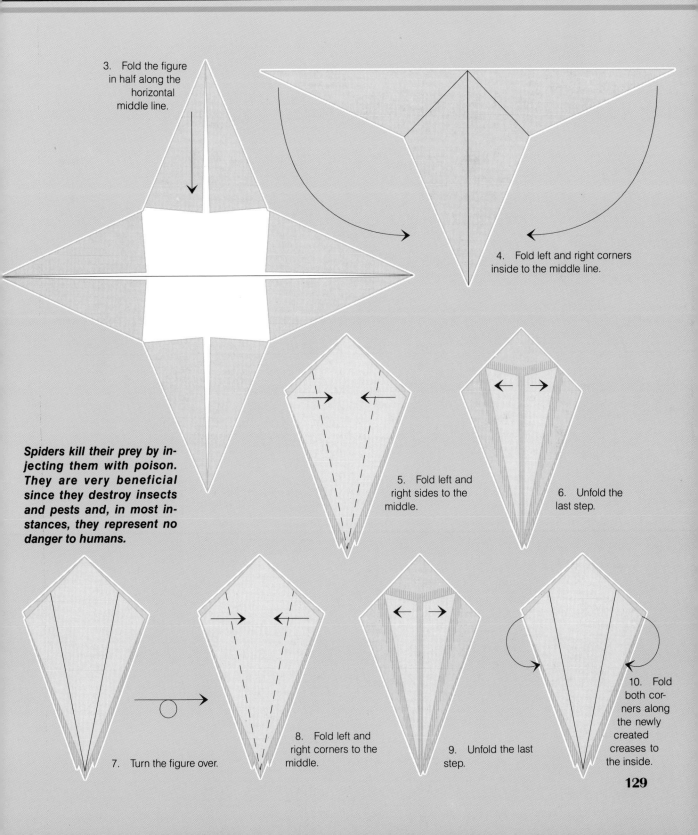

3.   Fold the figure in half along the horizontal middle line.

4.   Fold left and right corners inside to the middle line.

Spiders kill their prey by injecting them with poison. They are very beneficial since they destroy insects and pests and, in most instances, they represent no danger to humans.

5.   Fold left and right sides to the middle.

6.   Unfold the last step.

7.   Turn the figure over.

8.   Fold left and right corners to the middle.

9.   Unfold the last step.

10.   Fold both corners along the newly created creases to the inside.

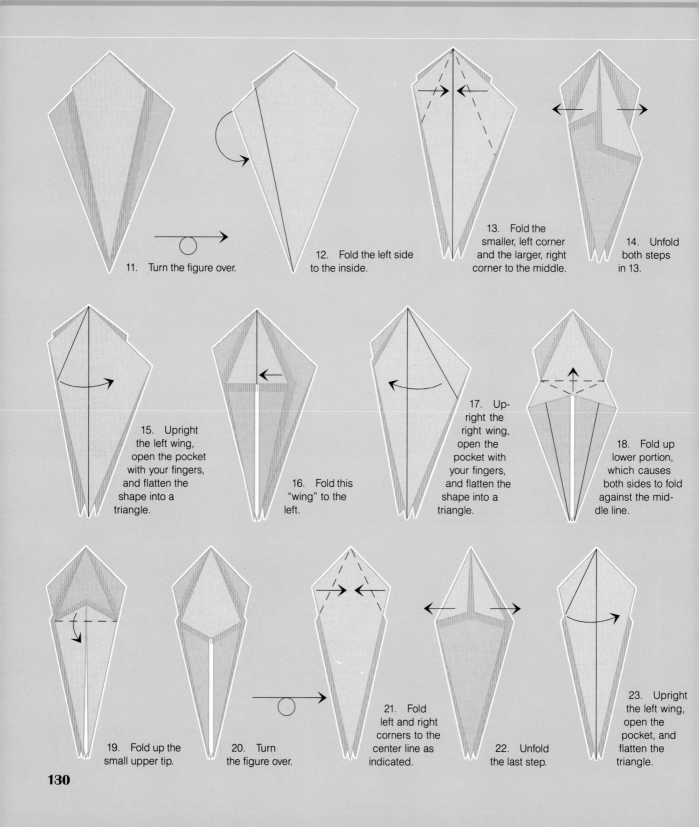

11. Turn the figure over.

12. Fold the left side to the inside.

13. Fold the smaller, left corner and the larger, right corner to the middle.

14. Unfold both steps in 13.

15. Upright the left wing, open the pocket with your fingers, and flatten the shape into a triangle.

16. Fold this "wing" to the left.

17. Upright the right wing, open the pocket with your fingers, and flatten the shape into a triangle.

18. Fold up lower portion, which causes both sides to fold against the middle line.

19. Fold up the small upper tip.

20. Turn the figure over.

21. Fold left and right corners to the center line as indicated.

22. Unfold the last step.

23. Upright the left wing, open the pocket, and flatten the triangle.

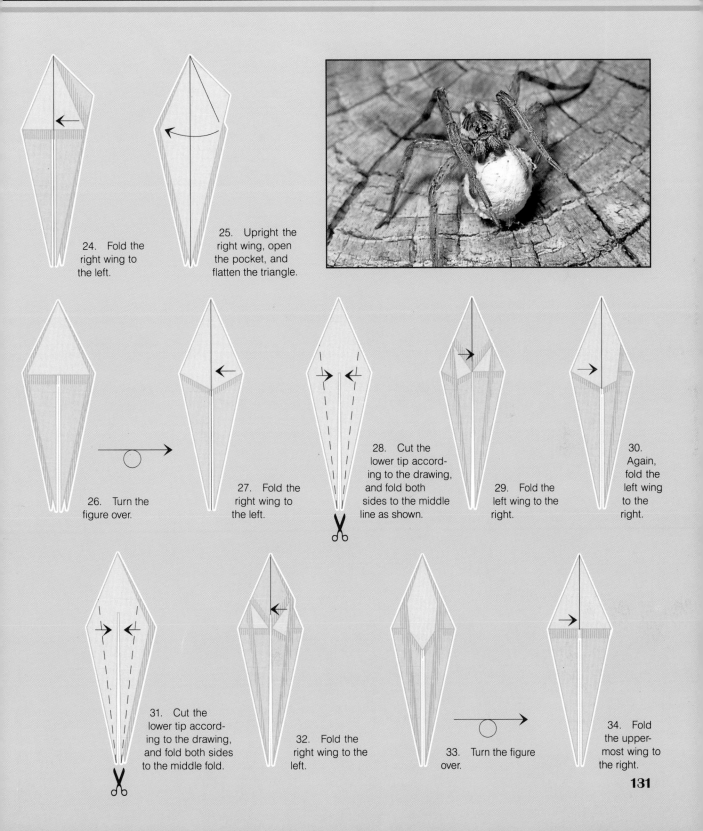

24. Fold the right wing to the left.

25. Upright the right wing, open the pocket, and flatten the triangle.

26. Turn the figure over.

27. Fold the right wing to the left.

28. Cut the lower tip according to the drawing, and fold both sides to the middle line as shown.

29. Fold the left wing to the right.

30. Again, fold the left wing to the right.

31. Cut the lower tip according to the drawing, and fold both sides to the middle fold.

32. Fold the right wing to the left.

33. Turn the figure over.

34. Fold the uppermost wing to the right.

131

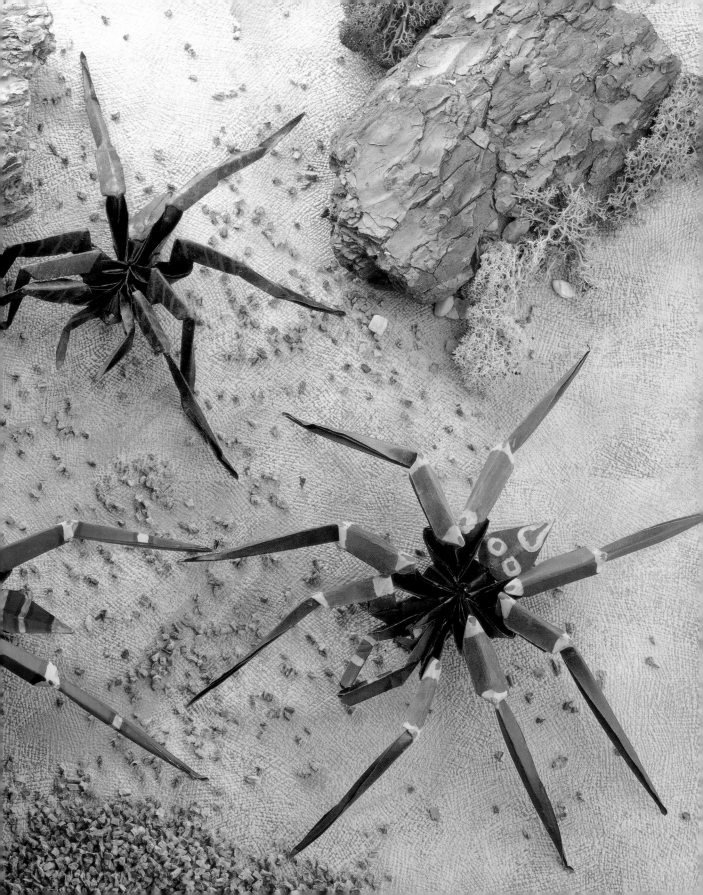

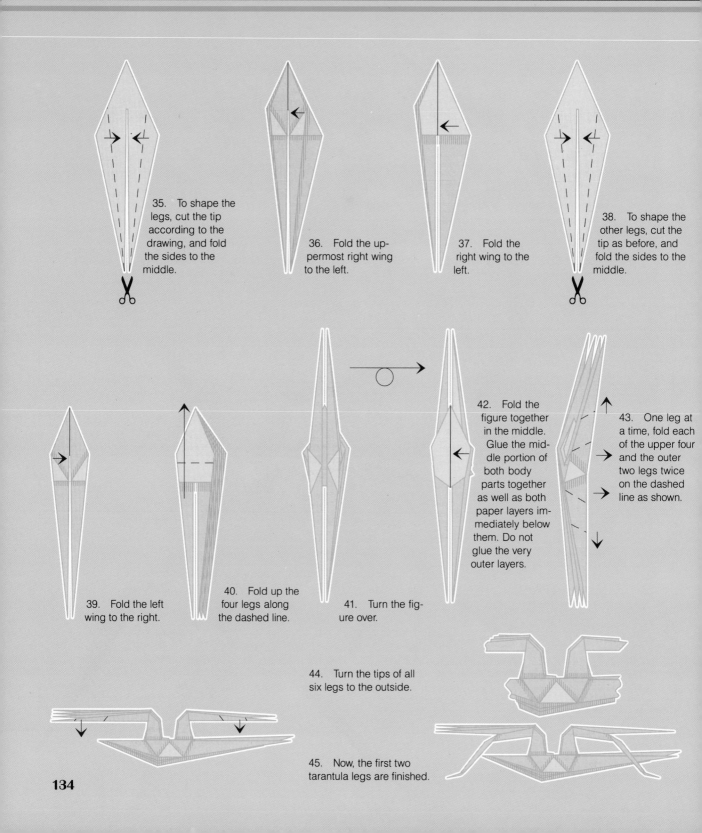

35. To shape the legs, cut the tip according to the drawing, and fold the sides to the middle.

36. Fold the uppermost right wing to the left.

37. Fold the right wing to the left.

38. To shape the other legs, cut the tip as before, and fold the sides to the middle.

39. Fold the left wing to the right.

40. Fold up the four legs along the dashed line.

41. Turn the figure over.

42. Fold the figure together in the middle. Glue the middle portion of both body parts together as well as both paper layers immediately below them. Do not glue the very outer layers.

43. One leg at a time, fold each of the upper four and the outer two legs twice on the dashed line as shown.

44. Turn the tips of all six legs to the outside.

45. Now, the first two tarantula legs are finished.

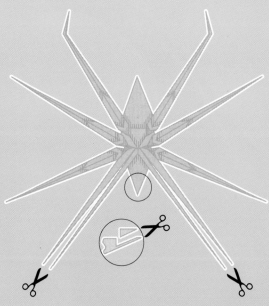

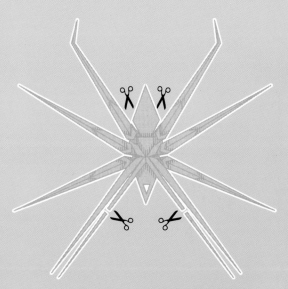

46. Cut to shape the head as in the detailed drawing in the circle.

47. Shorten the feelers just created, and turn them inside. Fold the remaining two tips into legs as described before. Cut the hindquarters as indicated and turn the figure upright into the horizontal position.

The most poisonous spider is the black widow, native to North and South America. The female is black with an hourglass-shaped red mark on the underside of her abdomen. Her bites can be life-threatening for animals as well as for humans.

The bite of the feared "bird spider" is not worse than a bee sting.

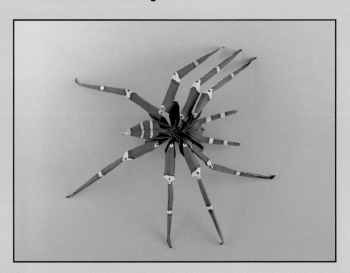

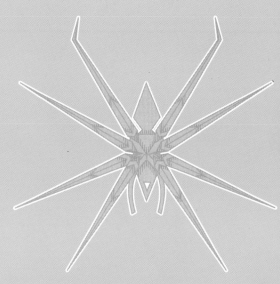

Beetles, with more than 350,000 different species, are by far the most numerous of the insect family, and they can be found everywhere on the globe. Beetles can be recognized by both the shape of the extension on the head and of their antennae, or "feelers," which they also use for smelling. Some beetles are blind; however, others are good at recognizing color. Most are herbivores and can be pests, like the May, potato, bark, and Japanese beetle. Others live on small insects and small animals and are, therefore, beneficial. Their ability to fly varies according to their habits. Often their legs are specialized for walking, jumping, digging, or swimming.

The rhinoceros beetle, a giant among beetles, is reddish brown to black and has a long, rhinoceros-like horn. This beetle grows up to 6 inches (15 centimetres) long and lives in the tropics and subtropics of the Americas and Eurasia. The European counterpart only reaches about 1½ inches (4 centimetres) in length.

Rhinoceros Beetle

1. Start by folding the Basic Form steps 1 to 11, and fold all 4 corners to the middle.

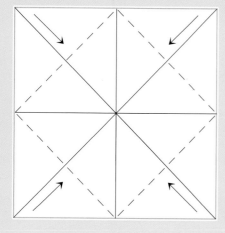

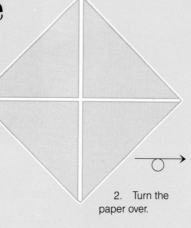

2. Turn the paper over.

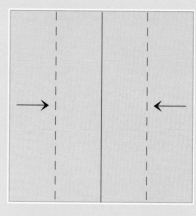

3. Fold the left and right sides along the dashed lines to the middle, letting the corners underneath extend at the sides.

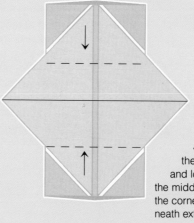

4. Fold the upper and lower sides to the middle, and let the corners underneath extend out.

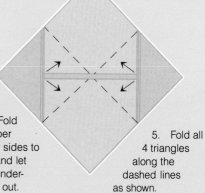

5. Fold all 4 triangles along the dashed lines as shown.

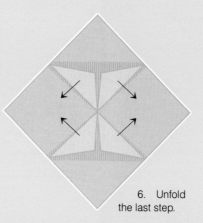

6. Unfold the last step.

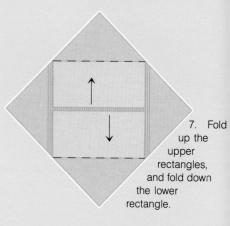

7. Fold up the upper rectangles, and fold down the lower rectangle.

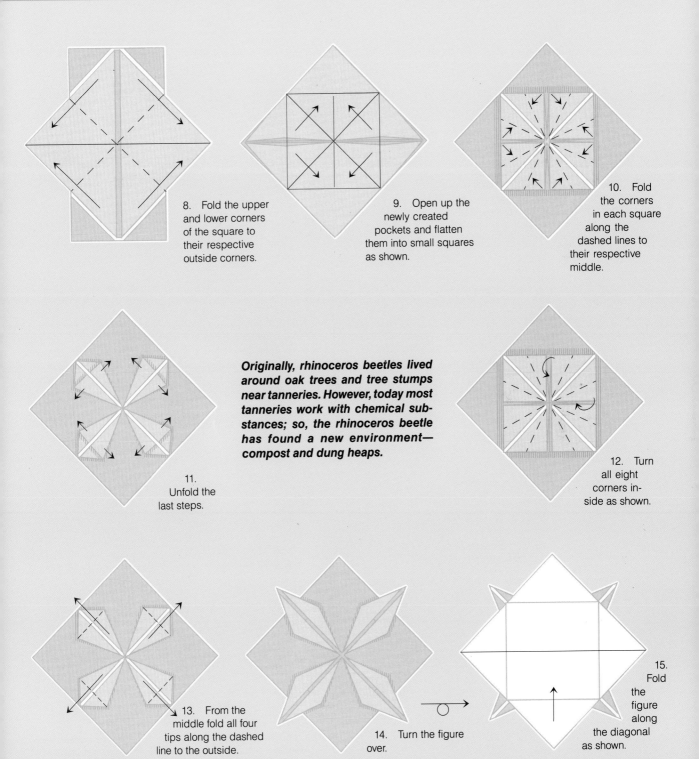

8. Fold the upper and lower corners of the square to their respective outside corners.

9. Open up the newly created pockets and flatten them into small squares as shown.

10. Fold the corners in each square along the dashed lines to their respective middle.

11. Unfold the last steps.

Originally, rhinoceros beetles lived around oak trees and tree stumps near tanneries. However, today most tanneries work with chemical substances; so, the rhinoceros beetle has found a new environment—compost and dung heaps.

12. Turn all eight corners inside as shown.

13. From the middle fold all four tips along the dashed line to the outside.

14. Turn the figure over.

15. Fold the figure along the diagonal as shown.

139

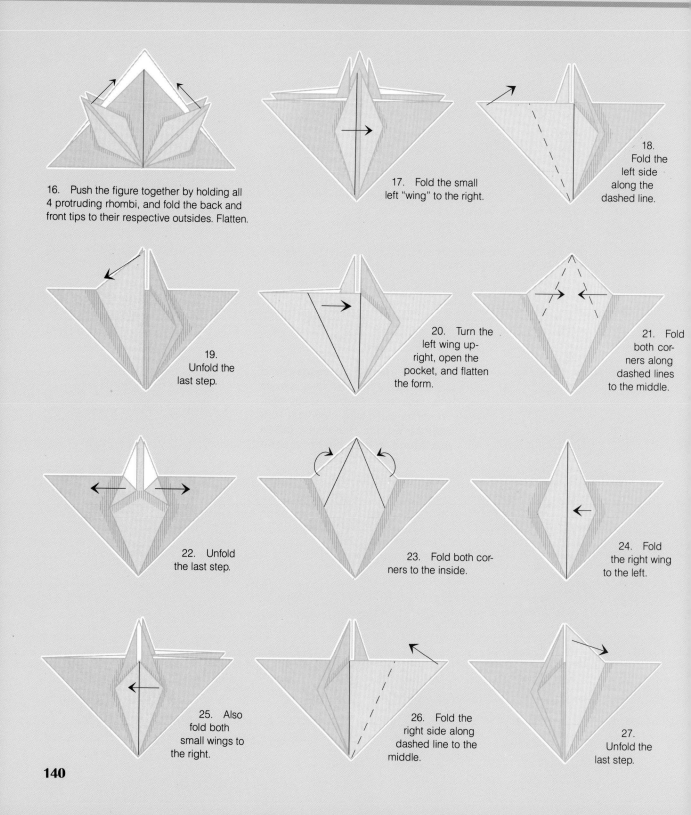

16. Push the figure together by holding all 4 protruding rhombi, and fold the back and front tips to their respective outsides. Flatten.

17. Fold the small left "wing" to the right.

18. Fold the left side along the dashed line.

19. Unfold the last step.

20. Turn the left wing upright, open the pocket, and flatten the form.

21. Fold both corners along dashed lines to the middle.

22. Unfold the last step.

23. Fold both corners to the inside.

24. Fold the right wing to the left.

25. Also fold both small wings to the right.

26. Fold the right side along dashed line to the middle.

27. Unfold the last step.

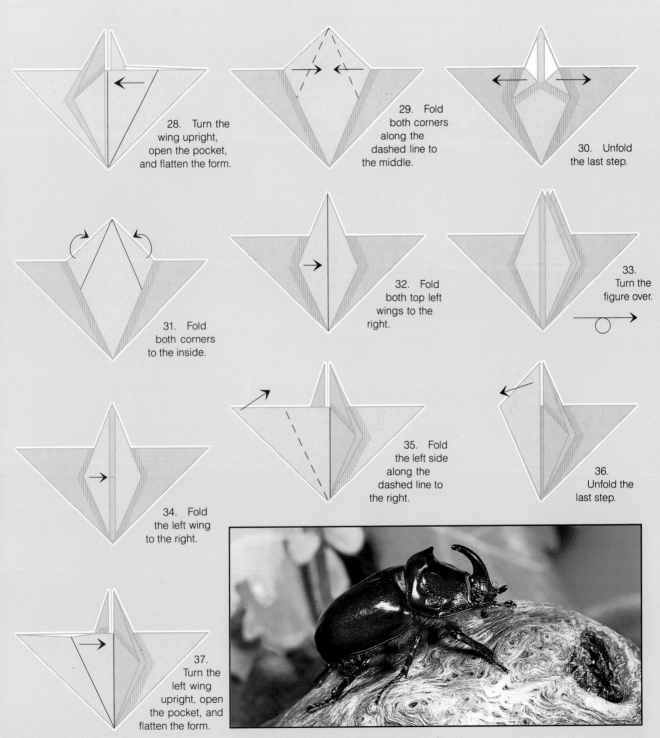

28. Turn the wing upright, open the pocket, and flatten the form.

29. Fold both corners along the dashed line to the middle.

30. Unfold the last step.

31. Fold both corners to the inside.

32. Fold both top left wings to the right.

33. Turn the figure over.

34. Fold the left wing to the right.

35. Fold the left side along the dashed line to the right.

36. Unfold the last step.

37. Turn the left wing upright, open the pocket, and flatten the form.

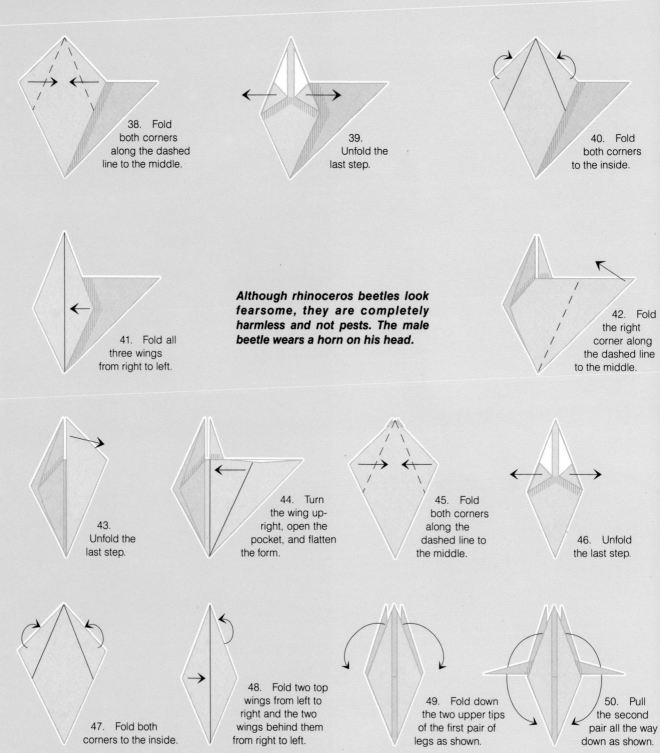

38. Fold both corners along the dashed line to the middle.

39. Unfold the last step.

40. Fold both corners to the inside.

41. Fold all three wings from right to left.

Although rhinoceros beetles look fearsome, they are completely harmless and not pests. The male beetle wears a horn on his head.

42. Fold the right corner along the dashed line to the middle.

43. Unfold the last step.

44. Turn the wing upright, open the pocket, and flatten the form.

45. Fold both corners along the dashed line to the middle.

46. Unfold the last step.

47. Fold both corners to the inside.

48. Fold two top wings from left to right and the two wings behind them from right to left.

49. Fold down the two upper tips of the first pair of legs as shown.

50. Pull the second pair all the way down as shown.

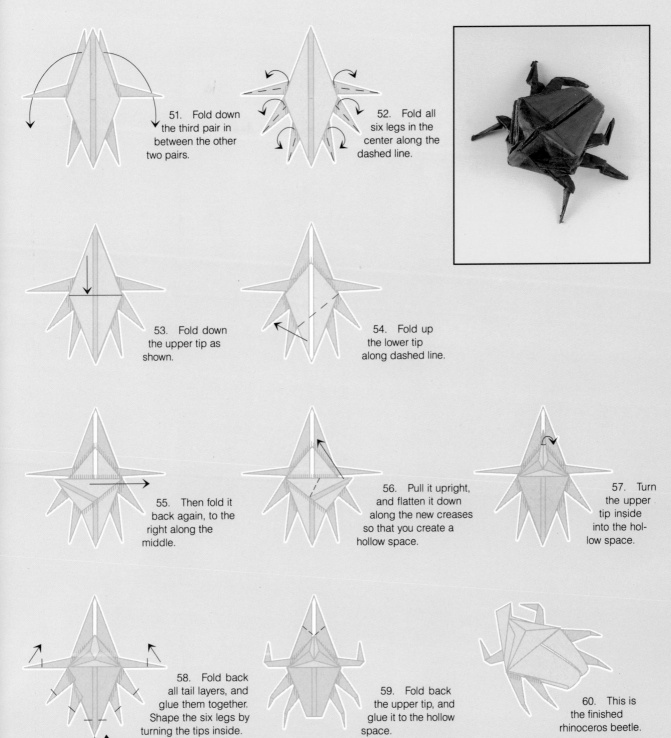

51. Fold down the third pair in between the other two pairs.

52. Fold all six legs in the center along the dashed line.

53. Fold down the upper tip as shown.

54. Fold up the lower tip along dashed line.

55. Then fold it back again, to the right along the middle.

56. Pull it upright, and flatten it down along the new creases so that you create a hollow space.

57. Turn the upper tip inside into the hollow space.

58. Fold back all tail layers, and glue them together. Shape the six legs by turning the tips inside.

59. Fold back the upper tip, and glue it to the hollow space.

60. This is the finished rhinoceros beetle.

Crabs and other crustaceans are gill-breathers, adapted to living in water. They always have more than 4 pairs of legs. These legs are used both for locomotion and as feelers that help orient the crab. Some legs also serve as jaws for snatching nourishment. Crabs frequently shed and regrow their skeletal plate (carapace or shell) that covers the fused head and thorax (cephalothorax). Crabs are often injured during this molting process, and they might even lose one of their legs. However, this does not matter since they easily regrow them. Over 40,000 different species of crustaceans live in the oceans as well as in freshwater lakes. Crustaceans date as far back as 600 million years. They reproduce by laying eggs, carried by the female in a breast pouch. Most crabs are not bigger than insects.

River crabs and lobsters are decapods and belong to the family of large crustaceans. The so-called pocket crab, weighing usually more than 11 pounds (5 kilograms), is the largest crab on the European coast.

Pocket Crab

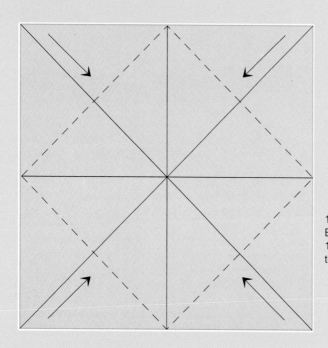

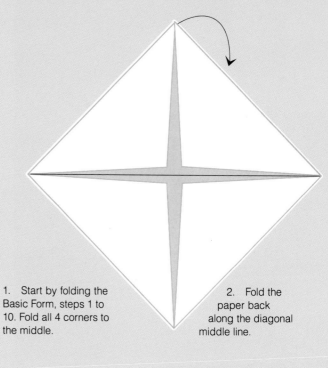

1. Start by folding the Basic Form, steps 1 to 10. Fold all 4 corners to the middle.

2. Fold the paper back along the diagonal middle line.

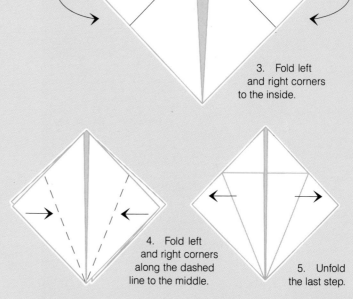

3. Fold left and right corners to the inside.

4. Fold left and right corners along the dashed line to the middle.

5. Unfold the last step.

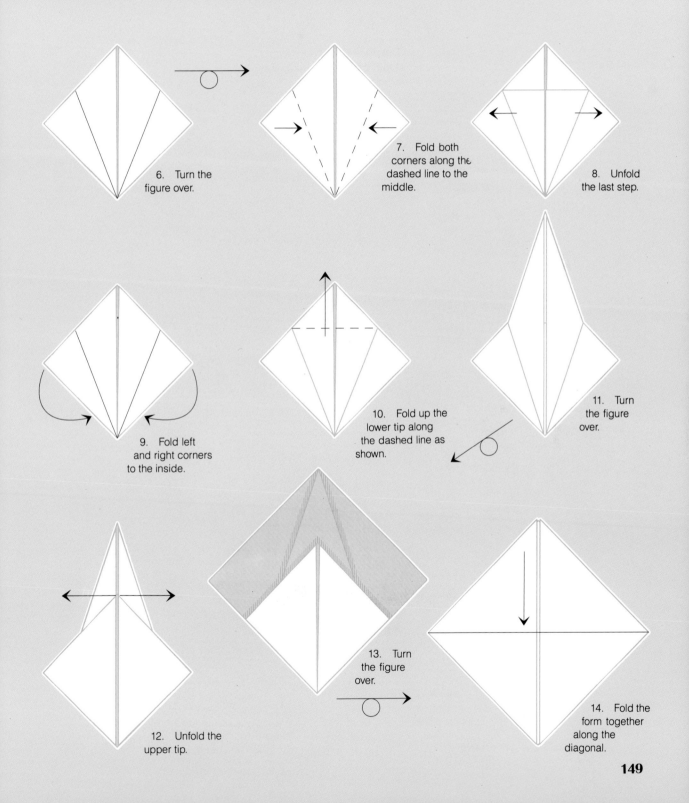

6. Turn the figure over.

7. Fold both corners along the dashed line to the middle.

8. Unfold the last step.

9. Fold left and right corners to the inside.

10. Fold up the lower tip along the dashed line as shown.

11. Turn the figure over.

12. Unfold the upper tip.

13. Turn the figure over.

14. Fold the form together along the diagonal.

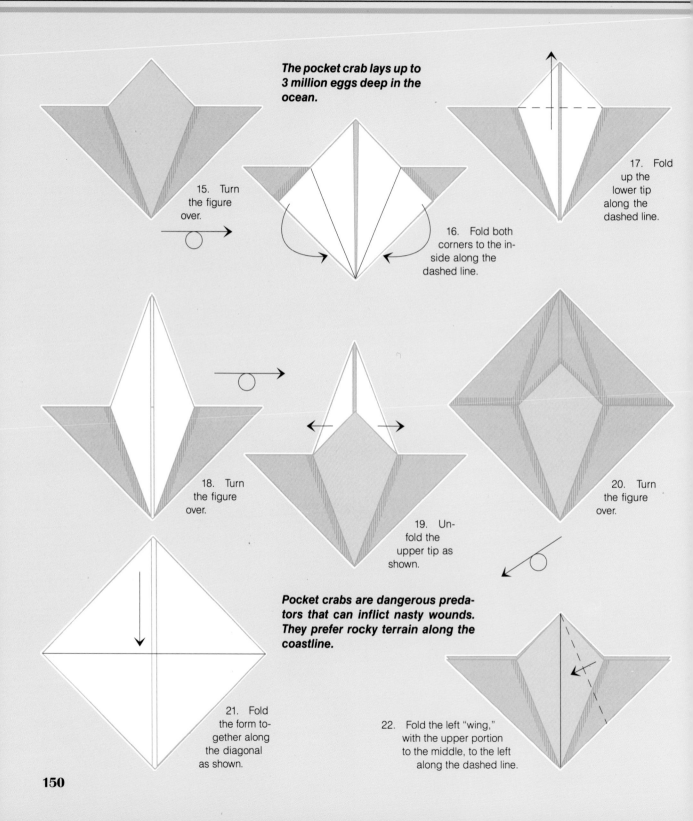

The pocket crab lays up to 3 million eggs deep in the ocean.

15. Turn the figure over.

16. Fold both corners to the inside along the dashed line.

17. Fold up the lower tip along the dashed line.

18. Turn the figure over.

19. Unfold the upper tip as shown.

20. Turn the figure over.

Pocket crabs are dangerous predators that can inflict nasty wounds. They prefer rocky terrain along the coastline.

21. Fold the form together along the diagonal as shown.

22. Fold the left "wing," with the upper portion to the middle, to the left along the dashed line.

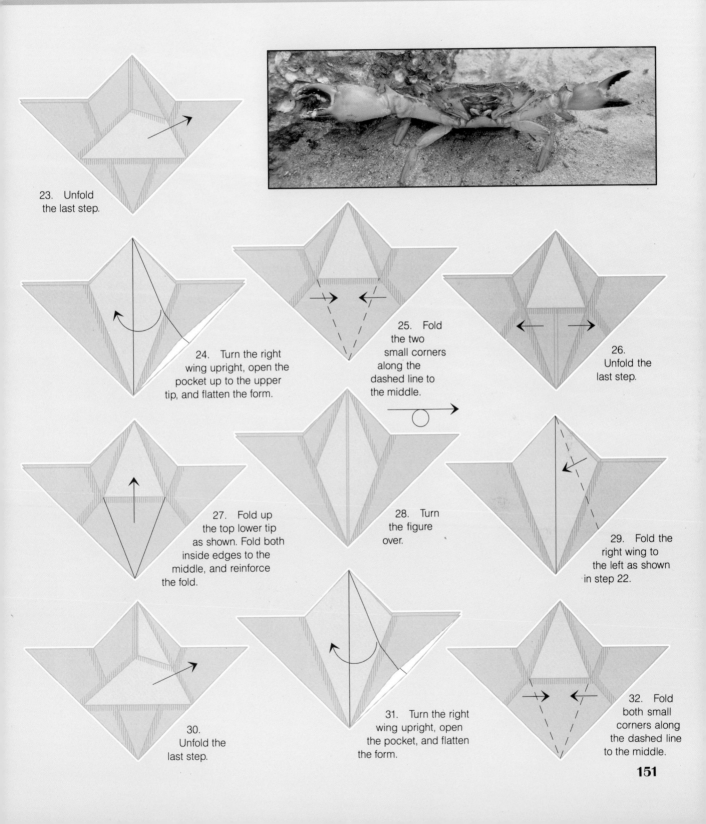

23. Unfold
the last step.

24. Turn the right
wing upright, open the
pocket up to the upper
tip, and flatten the form.

25. Fold
the two
small corners
along the
dashed line to
the middle.

26.
Unfold the
last step.

27. Fold up
the top lower tip
as shown. Fold both
inside edges to the
middle, and reinforce
the fold.

28. Turn
the figure
over.

29. Fold the
right wing to
the left as shown
in step 22.

30.
Unfold the
last step.

31. Turn the right
wing upright, open
the pocket, and flatten
the form.

32. Fold
both small
corners along
the dashed line
to the middle.

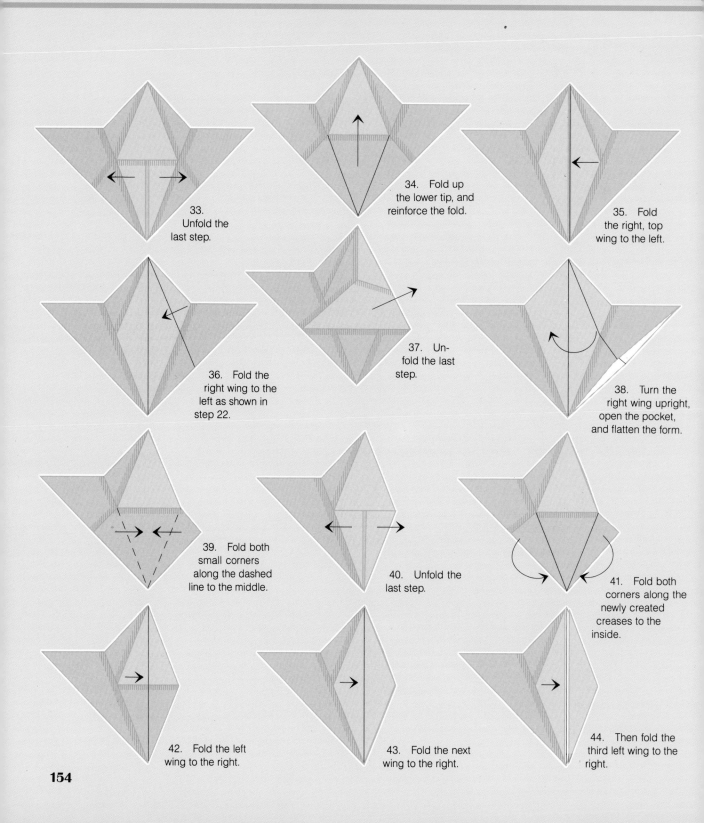

33. Unfold the last step.

34. Fold up the lower tip, and reinforce the fold.

35. Fold the right, top wing to the left.

36. Fold the right wing to the left as shown in step 22.

37. Unfold the last step.

38. Turn the right wing upright, open the pocket, and flatten the form.

39. Fold both small corners along the dashed line to the middle.

40. Unfold the last step.

41. Fold both corners along the newly created creases to the inside.

42. Fold the left wing to the right.

43. Fold the next wing to the right.

44. Then fold the third left wing to the right.

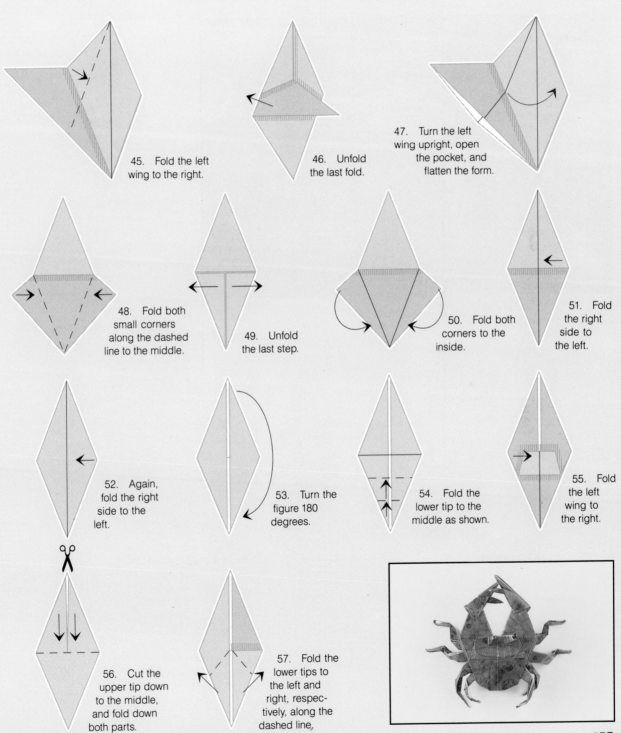

45. Fold the left wing to the right.

46. Unfold the last fold.

47. Turn the left wing upright, open the pocket, and flatten the form.

48. Fold both small corners along the dashed line to the middle.

49. Unfold the last step.

50. Fold both corners to the inside.

51. Fold the right side to the left.

52. Again, fold the right side to the left.

53. Turn the figure 180 degrees.

54. Fold the lower tip to the middle as shown.

55. Fold the left wing to the right.

56. Cut the upper tip down to the middle, and fold down both parts.

57. Fold the lower tips to the left and right, respectively, along the dashed line.

155

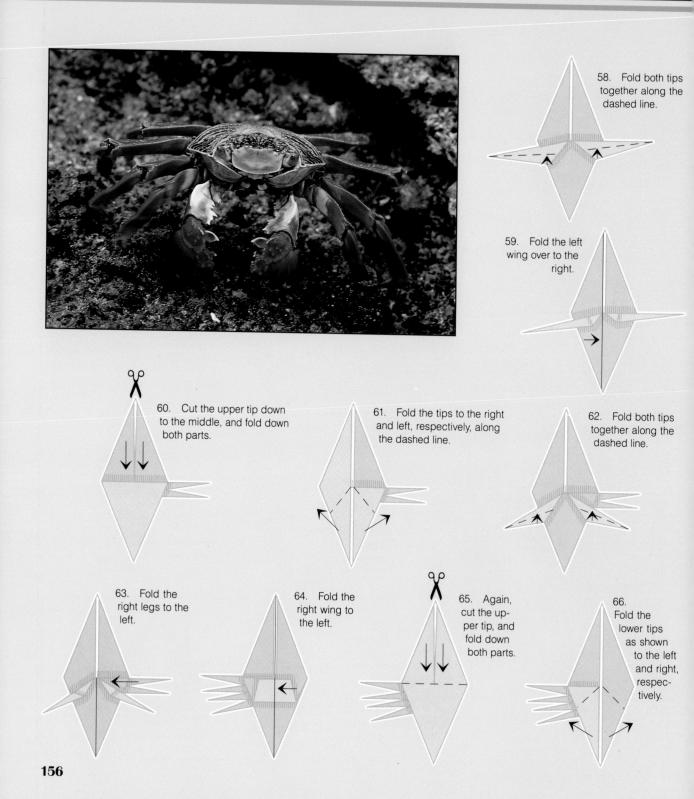

58. Fold both tips together along the dashed line.

59. Fold the left wing over to the right.

60. Cut the upper tip down to the middle, and fold down both parts.

61. Fold the tips to the right and left, respectively, along the dashed line.

62. Fold both tips together along the dashed line.

63. Fold the right legs to the left.

64. Fold the right wing to the left.

65. Again, cut the upper tip, and fold down both parts.

66. Fold the lower tips as shown to the left and right, respectively.

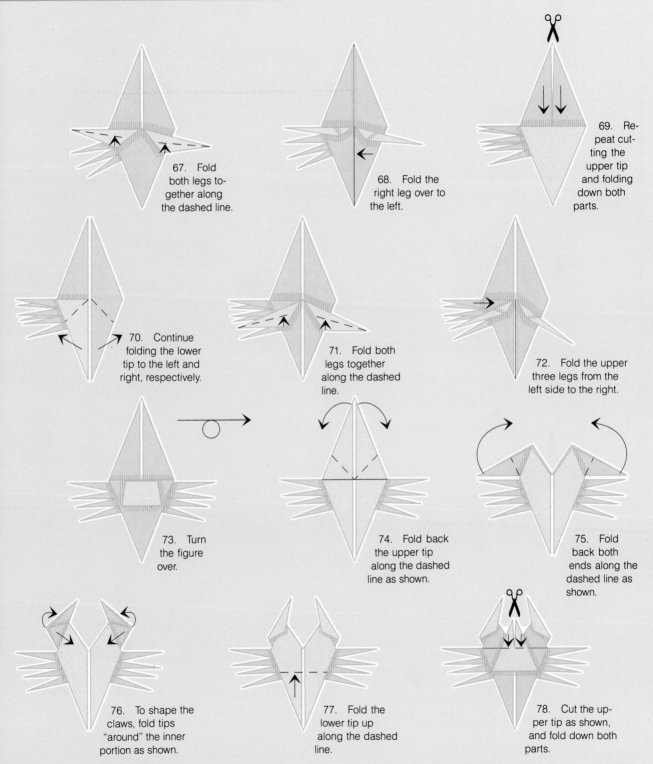

67. Fold both legs together along the dashed line.

68. Fold the right leg over to the left.

69. Repeat cutting the upper tip and folding down both parts.

70. Continue folding the lower tip to the left and right, respectively.

71. Fold both legs together along the dashed line.

72. Fold the upper three legs from the left side to the right.

73. Turn the figure over.

74. Fold back the upper tip along the dashed line as shown.

75. Fold back both ends along the dashed line as shown.

76. To shape the claws, fold tips "around" the inner portion as shown.

77. Fold the lower tip up along the dashed line.

78. Cut the upper tip as shown, and fold down both parts.

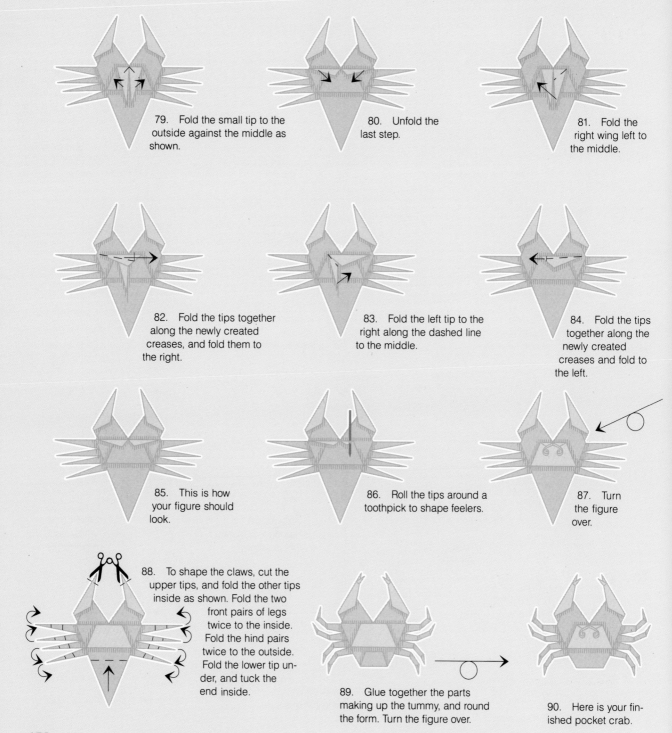

79. Fold the small tip to the outside against the middle as shown.

80. Unfold the last step.

81. Fold the right wing left to the middle.

82. Fold the tips together along the newly created creases, and fold them to the right.

83. Fold the left tip to the right along the dashed line to the middle.

84. Fold the tips together along the newly created creases and fold to the left.

85. This is how your figure should look.

86. Roll the tips around a toothpick to shape feelers.

87. Turn the figure over.

88. To shape the claws, cut the upper tips, and fold the other tips inside as shown. Fold the two front pairs of legs twice to the inside. Fold the hind pairs twice to the outside. Fold the lower tip under, and tuck the end inside.

89. Glue together the parts making up the tummy, and round the form. Turn the figure over.

90. Here is your finished pocket crab.

Index